Roller Coasters

Mike Schafer and Scott Rutherford

MBI Publishing Company

Dedication
To the memory of "Coaster Mike" Danshaw, the world's ultimate roller coaster fan

First published in 1998 by MBI Publishing Company, 729 Prospect Avenue, PO Box 1, Osceola, WI 54020-0001 USA

© Andover Junction Publications, 1998.

MBI Publishing Company books are also available at discounts in bulk quantity for industrial or sales-promotional use. For details write to Special Sales Manager at Motorbooks International Wholesalers & Distributors, PO Box 1, Osceola, WI 54020-0001 USA.

Library of Congress Cataloging-in-Publication Data Available

ISBN 0-7603-0506-4

On the front cover: Riders are either clinging to their lap bars or waving their arms in wild abandon as they thrill to the first drop of the venerable *Wild One* coaster at Adventure World park near Washington, D.C. The park opened in the 1980s, but major portions of this highly acclaimed coaster date from 1917 when it opened as the *Giant Coaster* at Paragon Park outside of Boston. That park closed, but Adventure World (formerly Wild World) purchased the elderly ride, moved it to Maryland, and revamped and reopened it. Such projects underscore an historic aspect of roller coasters—"the ultimate thrill ride." *Mike Schafer*

On the frontispiece: Anticipation is just one of many elements of a good roller-coaster ride, and this sign atop the lift hill of the *Giant Coaster* at Arnolds Park, Iowa, attests. *Terry Lind*

On the title page: The pure excitement of a roller coaster ride is captured in this view from the second seat of the blue train on the *Racer* at Paramount's Kings Island in Cincinnati as riders reach skyward while the red train (right side of photo) plunges into a significant lead. Regardless of which train returns to the loading station first, everyone will end up having a winning ride on the *Racer*—the coaster singularly credited as having sparked the roller coaster renaissance that began in 1972. *Mike Schafer*

On the back cover: Like a swirling art form high above the grounds of Busch Gardens Old Country in Williamsburg, Virginia, the new *Alpengeist* roller coaster flings riders through its famous "cobra roll" element. *Scott Rutherford*

Edited by Keith Mathiowetz
Designed by Katie L. Sonmor

Printed in Hong Kong through World Print, Ltd.

Contents

Acknowledgments

Any particular roller coaster may have a single designer, but you can bet that dozens of people were involved with its engineering, construction, marketing, and operation. The same is true of this book; I knew I couldn't do it all myself. To date I've ridden some 150 coasters, alive and defunct, but there are probably an equal number I haven't yet had a chance to sample. After all, the roller coaster boom that began in the 1970s has not subsided, and new coasters continue to spring up every season. So, my first thanks must go to co-author Scott Rutherford, who helped fill the voids. As longtime editor of *ACE News*, the newsletter of the American Coaster Enthusiasts (ACE), I knew Scott would be best for this job.

Together, Scott and I must thank Terry Lind of New York City for helping us fill a critical need for photos to round out this book's coaster coverage.

Likewise, applause also goes to Otto P. Dobnick of Waukesha, Wisconsin, for his photo contributions.

For additional assistance, I would like to thank Allen and Lucy Ambrosini, the publishers and editors of *At-The-Park* magazine. More than any two people, Allen and Lucy inspired my own renaissance in coastering. In addition, thanks must also go to Randy Rasmussen, Tom Halterman, and Dave and Jill Oroszi for their assistance and illustrative contributions.

As with all my book projects, a special thanks for support goes to Joyce Mooney and Steve Esposito, my partners and friends within our own company, Andover Junction Publications, the producer of this book. As well, we appreciate the support and enthusiasm of the folks at MBI Publishing Company, the publisher of this book.

—Mike Schafer
Lee, Illinois

Introduction

My fascination with roller coasters dates from my preschool years. I still have a color-crayon drawing of a roller coaster that I did in 1955 as a first-grader at Wight School in Rockford, Illinois. Interestingly, at the time, I had never seen a coaster in the flesh (or wood, or steel, if you will), but I *had* seen them on TV and in the movies, and they left quite an impression on me. A few years later, my grandmother took my sister and me to Chicago to "ride" the *Atom Smasher* coaster featured in one of the movies playing at the Cinerama—the surround-screen movie theater that was the talk of the Midwest.

If someone had told me then that someday I would actually ride the *Atom Smasher*, at now-defunct Rockaway Playland near New York City, I would have been thrilled beyond words. As it was, I was growing up in nearly a coaster void. My hometown amusement park had only a little steel kiddie coaster. I yearned to see and ride a real, full-size, wooden coaster.

Early in the 1960s, I began listening to WLS radio (AM 890) beaming from Chicago, 85 miles away. Commercials featuring Chicago's Riverview Park and its legendary *Bobs* roller coaster were staples of summertime listening. Finally, in 1967, four of us high school seniors made a pilgrimage to Riverview where I lost my wooden-coaster virginity to (bow in reverence, please) the *Bobs*. I was hooked.

Alas, my coaster conquests went into hibernation when Riverview Park closed later that year. Without any other nearby coasters—and certainly without other people to share my strange fixation with coasters—my coaster endeavors went into a low ebb. . . until 1971, when I discovered Denver's Elitch Gardens and was astounded by a ride on *Mister Twister*—a ride which changed my life. *Mister Twister* told me there *was* coaster life beyond Riverview, and that some coasters were even more wild than the *Bobs*.

Still, I couldn't find anyone who shared my coaster obsession, and I still had few clues as to where there were other parks with coasters. The turning point came in 1978 when I joined a new club that had been formed exclusively for deranged folks who lived, breathed, and rode roller coasters: the American Coaster Enthusiasts (ACE), an energetic, eclectic, fun-loving group of coasterholics who not only loved riding coasters, but knew where *every* one of 'em was. Nirvana! In short time, they

Coaster evolution—in particular the emergence of the tubular steel-track coaster in the late 1950s—has resulted in rides of unprecedented acrobatics, graphically illustrated in this scene of Kentucky Kingdom's new (1995) T^2 (*Terror to the Second Power*) coaster in action. T^2 is a radical "inverted" (overhead-track) coaster which turns riders upside down five times through a variety of track configurations that a half century earlier would have been thought impossible. *Terry Lind*

made me part of the "family," invited me to coaster parties, and swept me along on coaster hunts. Throughout the 1980s, my coaster experiences soared, thanks to ACE.

All of this leads me to the main point of this introduction. *Roller Coasters* cuts to the quick. You won't have to wonder like I did if there are others out there (there are scads) who have a bizarre fascination for a device that many consider to be sheer madness. Nor will you have to spend years like I did trying to figure out where coasters lurk. We've taken care of that right here in the pages of this book.

A few caveats before the lap bar comes down. First, this volume is not meant to be the all-comprehensive, see-all, end-all book on roller coasters. If you want to get into some serious coaster research, we heartily recommend *The Incredible Scream Machine: A History of the Roller Coaster*, by Robert Cartmell (Fairview Park, Ohio: Amusement Park Books, Inc. and Bowling Green Ohio: Bowling Green State University Popular Press, 1987). You also won't regret joining the American Coaster Enthusiasts, P.O. Box 8226, Chicago, IL 60680. ACE publishes a quarterly magazine, *Roller Coaster*; a newsletter; detailed coaster guides; and

also hosts conventions and conferences at parks throughout North America.

Space restrictions prevent us from covering "stock" portable or semi-portable roller coasters (e.g., *Galaxies*, *Jumbo Jets*, *Hurricanes*) often found at large fairs and traveling carnivals, even if they have become "permanent" installations at regular parks. For purposes of this book—and again because of space considerations—we are including only U.S. coasters that meet the following criteria: the ride must have wheeled cars or trains that move by gravity throughout most of a continuous, closed-circuit track. Regretfully, this leaves out "coaster cousins" such as log flume rides, free-falls, and, most notably, shuttle-loop-type coasters.

Although we've been careful to make sure that the rides herein were up and running as of press time, rides can be taken out of service unexpectedly and indefinitely or even dismantled. Check with a park regarding ride status (as well as the park operating schedule) before you spend time and money traveling to the park.

Each ride description includes the coaster name, year built, type of coaster, height of the highest lift hill, and length of track run. Our ride descriptions may differ from your own experiences. Keep in mind that the ride quality of roller coasters—especially wooden ones—varies with weather conditions, the time of day (most are faster toward the end of the day), and other factors.

Above all, have fun!

—*Mike Schafer*

1

Our Roller Coaster HERITAGE

The gravity thrill ride that is today the centerpiece of amusement parks is largely an American phenomenon, but the roller coaster's roots date from fifteenth century Russia. They weren't really "coasters" as we know them now, of course. Rather, they were ice-covered slides built for winter amusement. Thrill-seekers hiked up wooden stairs to the top, then boarded sleds to whoosh down the ramp at the mercy of gravity.

These ice slides became enormously popular (and dangerous, which added to their popularity), and their construction grew more sophisticated and ornate over the decades. Eventually they became known as "Russian Mountains," and the ice-slide phenomenon caught on in surrounding countries.

Signs reflect the tantalizing variety of roller coasters found across the United States—rides that evolved from the simple, sometimes nameless, coasters that began appearing in America toward the end of the nineteenth century. *Thunderbolt*, Riverside Park, Massachusetts, *Terry Lind*; *Cannon Ball*, Lake Winnepesaukah, Georgia; *Racer* and *Dipper*, Kennywood Park, Pennsylvania; *Comet Flyer*, Whalom Park, Massachusetts; *Screamin' Eagle*, Six Flags Mid-America, Missouri; *Z-Force*, Great America, Illinois; *Big Bad Wolf*, Busch Gardens, Virginia. *Otto P. Dobnick. (Mike Schafer photos except as noted.)*

One of the popular predecessors to the modern, high-speed roller coaster was the *Scenic Railway*, developed by La Marcus Thompson. The *Scenic Railway* featured gentle dips (though at the time considered radical) and scenic—sometimes partially enclosed—surroundings. The popularity of the *Scenic Railway* spread throughout U.S. amusement parks. This early twentieth-century tinted postcard showed the *Scenic Railway* at famous Euclid Beach park in Cleveland. *Mike Schafer Collection*

The Russians can also be credited with adding wheels to the sleds, thereby creating the first true roller coaster circa 1784 and allowing them to become a year-round pastime. Early in the nineteenth century, France became a hotbed of coaster development, with coaster rides erected as early as 1804 and coasters with cars that were locked to tracks (the essence of safe coastering today) appearing in 1817. By mid-century, looping coasters had even debuted, though accidents and technical problems soon rendered upside-down coastering unpopular—at least for the ensuing 125 years.

COASTERS COME TO THE NEW WORLD

Amazingly, the largest and longest roller coaster ever built in North America was also the first, the *Gravity Road* at Mauch Chunk (now Jim Thorpe), Pennsylvania. Built in 1827, the original function of the winding, point-to-point railroad was to move coal from a mine at the top of Mount Pisgah down to boats on the Lehigh Canal. The railway's average grade was more than 1.5 percent, so trains of coal cars could roll downhill via gravity. A brake operator on each train kept it from getting out of control. Once the coal cars were unloaded, mules retraced the route, hauling the

Forest Park, Giant Safety Coaster.
The most elaborate and largest coaster in the United States.

The modern "high-speed" roller coaster debuted in 1907 at Coney Island in Brooklyn, New York. Featuring higher lift hills, steeper and deeper drops, and higher speeds than figure-eighters and *Scenic Railways*, this new breed of coaster caught on quickly. This postcard postmarked June 8, 1909, shows the high-speed *Giant Safety Coaster*—"The most elaborate and largest coaster in the United States"—at Chicago's Forest Park. Because the advent of underfriction wheels was still three years away, this and most other coasters of the early twentieth century were of "side-friction" variety, with high side rails to keep coaster cars on course. *Mike Schafer Collection*

Amusement Grounds,
Washington Park,
Michigan City, Ind.

Making their appearance around the turn of the century, figure-eight coasters more or less followed the *Scenic Railway* in coaster evolution. Figure-eight coasters were all the rage during the first decade or so of the twentieth century, and every park worth their name had one. This postcard, postmarked July 24, 1916, featured the figure-eight coaster at Washington Park in Michigan City, Indiana. Only one vintage figure-eighter survives in North America, the *Leap-the-Dips* at Lakemont Park near Altoona, Pennsylvania. *Mike Schafer Collection*

13

The king of coaster designers during the Roarin' Twenties was John A. Miller. His signature design element was "camelback hump" hills which usually dipped all the way to the ground. Such hills are very much in evidence in this scene taken from aboard the Miller-designed *Coaster* at Riverview Park in Des Moines, Iowa, in 1978 just before the park closed for good. *Mike Schafer*

empty cars back up to the mine. The engineering marvel captured public fancy, and soon the *Gravity Road* was also providing rides for tourists.

In 1845, the railroad revised its trackage, adding incline planes to make operation more efficient. Now after unloading at Mauch Chunk, the empty cars were hoisted up a steep (nearly 30 percent grade) 2,322-foot incline to the mines via cable. After loading, the cars worked their way down to Mauch Chunk largely via the old *Gravity Road* route. Now known as the *Mauch Chunk Switchback*, it had an 18-mile continuous-circuit operation. Throngs stood in line for the breathtaking experience. Presto! A roller coaster had been born. Amazingly, the railway lasted until 1938, and its right of way—some 20 miles from Dorney Park, Allentown—can still be seen.

More than any one person, La Marcus A. Thompson (1848–1919) can be credited with *popularizing* the roller coaster and its kin—mainly the scenic railway—in North America. Inspired by the *Mauch Chunk Switchback*, Thompson was the first person to build a roller coaster expressly for public entertainment, opening his *Switchback Railway* at Coney Island in 1884.

It was a simple device: Passengers climbed a 50-foot loading station and boarded a train. Once released, the train wheeled by gravity along a 600-foot track of mildly undulating hills until it coasted to a stop. Passengers disembarked while attendants pushed the car uphill to another platform where the passengers reboarded for the return trip along a second track, onto which the train had been switched.

The ride caught on like wildfire, and soon *Switchback Railways* were appearing at amusement parks throughout the land. Other entrepreneurs got on the bandwagon, building their own coaster-like rides and incorporating improvements such as mechanical car hoists and continuous-circuit track layout, thus departing from the "switchback" format. In fact, track layouts began to take daring twists, and soon figure-eight patterns became immensely popular.

Prompted by competition, Thompson struck a new path in coasterdom when he opened the *Scenic Railway* in Atlantic City, New Jersey, in 1887. In essence, it drew upon the format popularized by other builders: a continuous track circuit with mechanically operated lift hills. However, there was a major difference with the *Scenic Railway*: it reflected Thompson's strong belief that coasters were sightseeing devices. Thus, his *Scenic Railways* featured complex artificial scenery, intricate lighting, and special effects such as dioramas.

The *Scenic Railway* was an immense success, spurring Thompson to form the L. A. Thompson Scenic Railway Company, which went on to build *Scenic Railways* all over the world. The concept survives today in such rides as Disneyland's *Matterhorn Bobsled* and numerous mine-train-themed rides.

At about the same time, another gravity ride emerged which mimicked toboggan sleds, but in place of snow were fixed guideways equipped with hundreds of rollers. Toboggan sleds, hoisted to the top of the run by an elevator, were released onto the track to coast down along the rollers. The best-known toboggan ride was the *Sliding-Hill and Toboggan* in Haverhill, Massachusetts. Opened in 1887, the ride—housed in a building above a skating rink—was designed by Stephen Jackman and Byron Floyd.

Some believe that the term "roller coaster" originated with the two entrepreneurs, although Thompson's 1885 patent for his switchback railway was titled "Roller Coasting Structure." Regardless, the toboggan format, like the *Scenic Railway* and switchback coasters, found wide appeal and proliferated in other parts of the U.S.

AMUSEMENT PARKS AND THEIR ROLLER COASTERS

Roller coaster evolution was closely intertwined with that of the amusement park. The latter was an outgrowth of the picnic grove, thousands of which populated nearly all settled areas of the U.S. by the turn of the century. The development of the American amusement park can also be traced to Europe, where "pleasure parks" had been a way of life since the seventeenth century. Pleasure parks offered entertainment to the masses, with bowling, archery, shuffleboard, singing, dancing, and circus-type acts. Refreshment areas, including "beer gardens," rounded out the festivities. Eventually, crude Ferris-type wheels, carousels, donkey rides, and such appeared, adding more pleasure to pleasure parks.

Under Herbert Schmeck—once an assistant to John Miller—the Philadelphia Toboggan Company (P.T.C.) became the premier U.S. coaster builder. Among P.T.C.'s legacy of stellar rides was the fearsome *Wildcat* at now-defunct Idora Park in Youngstown, Ohio. Built in 1930, the remarkable ride, shown from aboard a train on the lift hill in 1979, featured a vicious fan curve (opposite end in photo) that probably cracked more ribs than any other coaster of the Coaster Boom era that began in 1972. Sadly, Idora and its *Wildcat* and *Jack Rabbit* coasters closed in the 1980s, but P.T.C. remains an active force in new coaster construction. *Mike Schafer*

On American soil, one of the first large amusement parks of the pleasure park genre was Jones Woods in New York City, but its relatively early death (1860s) paved the way for a newer entertainment area nearby whose fame as a symbol of American fun endures to the present: Coney Island. Coney's wide, sandy beach on the Atlantic Ocean was the initial draw, but it quickly evolved into a bawdy entertainment area rife with vaudeville shows, billiard parlors, hotels, dance pavilions, beer halls, bathhouses, and eateries.

Eventually, individual amusement parks sprung up at Coney Island, one of the earliest being Sea Lion Park (1895) and one of the most famous being Steeplechase Park (1897). These were followed by two spectacular new parks: Luna Park, opened in 1903 and—lit by one million light bulbs—Dreamland in 1904. All of these parks incorporated some form of roller coaster, including the *Flip Flap* looping coaster, which debuted at Sea Lion in 1895.

The *Flip Flap* incorporated a true circle, which, because of its small diameter, caused severe discomfort to passengers' necks, but another looping coaster that appeared at Coney Island in 1901 solved the problem. The *Loop the Loop* utilized elliptical loops, which made the ride much more comfortable. Both rides were short-lived, but they can be considered the forerunners of the steel-looping coasters that today dominate the coaster world.

To Coney Island goes yet another coaster distinction: birthplace of the first high-speed roller coaster. Until Christopher Feucht opened his *Drop-the-Dip* in 1907 at

Coaster Technology

WHAT MAKES COASTERS GO?

Gravity, and little else, makes coasters go. The only mechanical propulsion involved is that which lifts coaster trains to the crest of a "lift hill." Beyond that, gravity takes over and trains make their descents, gaining enough momentum and energy to carry them through the rest of the ride. As a matter of physics, all hills following a lift hill must be smaller (although not necessarily successively smaller) than the lift hill or the coaster train will not be able to surmount them. To do so would require more energy than the train began with. Steepness of descents and ascents, as well as friction along the track, plays into the equations which determine just how high any of the hills can be and how long the track run can be. This Dorney Park (Allentown, Pennsylvania) Coaster train is racing along the speed bump following the lift hill; it has more than enough energy to take it through the raised backturn section partially visible beyond the trees.

Mike Schafer photo

Coney, roller coasters and *Scenic Railways* sported gentle hills and wide, slow turns. *Drop-the-Dip* ignored convention and went for the throat (or stomach, as the case may have been) with steep drops and tight turns that induced terror among riders—but not enough to keep them from riding. *Drop-the-Dip* was an instant hit, and other coaster builders soon followed suit, each trying to outdo the other with devious track plans and steep drops. The modern roller coaster had been born.

THE GOLDEN AGE OF ROLLER COASTERS

If nothing else, Coney Island at the turn of the century was a proving ground that the masses loved amusement parks and roller coasters. New parks (and coasters, of course) sprung up throughout America, and soon any city worthy of its name sported at least one major amusement park. Of course, nearly all the new parks featured some sort of coaster, while older picnic parks began to add them. Figure-eight coasters, toboggan rides, and *Scenic Railways* yielded to more turbulent coasters. The growing popularity of coasters prompted the formation of several coaster-building companies, behind which were individuals with a penchant for coaster design and development. One man in particular was critical to the rise of the roller coaster as the ultimate amusement ride: John A. Miller.

Born in 1872, Miller during his teen years was already working with coasters—and coaster pioneer La Marcus Thompson. Miller is best known for a number of coaster-related patents that greatly enhanced a coaster's safety and yet allowed for wilder, larger, and faster coasters. Chief among his devices were "underfriction wheels," patented in 1912. Underfriction wheels "lock" coaster trains to their tracks, preventing them from leaping off on curves or hilltops. He also developed locking bars to keep riders from flying out of their seats as a result of negative gravitational forces (negative Gs) induced by high-speed flights over hilltops. Virtually every coaster operating today, including the newest creations, incorporate Miller-inspired safety devices. Next time you ride a coaster and negative Gs thrust you up against the safety bar, thank John Miller that the

Despite an overall decline in coaster population and parks during the 1960s, there were a few bright spots. One was the opening of [*Mister*] *Twister* at Elitch Gardens in Denver in 1965; designed by P.T.C.'s John Allen, it was extensively rebuilt for the 1966 season, and for the next 30-plus years, *Twister* consistently reigned as one of the top five best coasters in North America. This view of *Twister* was taken from the *Wildcat*, a 1926 Schmeck/P.T.C. coaster whose trackage *Twister* intertwined. *Twister*'s calling card was its heavily banked, high-speed double helix. Both coasters were closed in 1996 when Elitch's moved across town. *Mike Schafer*

coaster train didn't fly off the track—nor you completely out of the car!

Miller consulted for other coaster builders, and from 1920 to 1923 joined forces with Harry C. Baker, forming Miller & Baker Inc. which collaborated on numerous wooden roller coasters. Both parties went off on their own after 1923, with Miller forming the John A. Miller Company. To his dying day in 1941, Miller was involved in coaster design and development, and his genius is underscored by the fact that one can still ride Miller-designed coasters. Baker's ensuing coaster career was less ambitious, but noteworthy nonetheless: His company constructed, in 1927, what is arguably the world's most famous roller coaster, Vernon Keenan's legendary Coney Island *Cyclone*.

A number of coaster designers, some of them freelancers (John Miller among them), did work for larger
continued on page 22

oaster design grew more radical as the 1920s drew to a close, and it was during this period that the *Cyclone* at Crystal Beach in Ontario (near Buffalo, New York) was unveiled by legendary coaster designer Harry Traver in 1927. Frequently billed as the most terrifying roller coaster ever to rule the earth, the *Cyclone* was a wood-track but steel-supported coaster with a brutally twisting, plunging track. A nurse was stationed at the unloading platform at the behest of insurance companies. In this 1943 view, a *Cyclone* train has just entered its pitching helix section. The coaster's reputation got the better of it, and the ride was dismantled after World War II, some of its steel supporting members being used on Crystal Beach's new *Comet*, which opened in 1947 and can be ridden today in Lake George, New York. *William C. Bryson, Mike Schafer Collection*

The Prior & Church Company (P.&C.) is credited with building some of the wildest—yet very rideable—coasters built during the first half of the twentieth century. Among Fred Church's longer-lived masterpieces (Thomas Prior kept to the business end of things) was the *Tornado* coaster at Coney Island, opened in 1926. It featured a compact and very convoluted track layout—a hallmark of P.&C. coasters. The ride is shown in 1975, two years before it was razed. *Tom Halterman*

The era of traditional parks was on the wane when this scene of Cincinnati's beautiful Coney Island was recorded in the spring of 1970. At right are the boarding station and part of the structure of the *Shooting Star,* while in the distance stands the *Wildcat.* Coney Island was actually enjoying increased popularity at this time, but was a frequent victim of Ohio River flooding. The park closed at the end of the 1970 season and was in part reincarnated in the new Kings Island theme park nearby. Ironically, both Coney coasters were replicated at three new theme parks in the 1980s, but not at Kings Island. *David P. Oroszi*

continued from page 19

amusement ride companies, and in one instance a former co-worker of Miller turned a fledgling firm into a chief rival of the John A. Miller Company. That man was Herb Schmeck, and the firm he took over was the Philadelphia Toboggan Company (P.T.C.). The company was formed in 1904, and nearly 95 years later, it is still involved in coaster design and construction. During those years, P.T.C. created some of the finest roller coasters of all time.

Meanwhile, Miller formed an alliance with National Amusement Devices (N.A.D.) of Dayton, Ohio. N.A.D. rose to prominence during the coaster-building boom of the Roaring Twenties. Though N.A.D. built several coasters, the company (later known as International Amusement Devices) is best-known for its classic, headlight-equipped Century Flyer coaster trains, several of which still ply the tracks of U.S. coasters.

For sheer coaster terror, two coaster designers top the list: Harry Traver and Frederick Church. Traver's Crystal Beach (Ontario) *Cyclone* has long purported to be the most terrifying, gut-wrenching coaster ever devised. The *Cyclone* opened in 1927 and featured a nurse's station for victims of its vicious tangle of trackage. Rising insurance premiums resulted in its dismantling shortly after World War II, its steel-supporting components reused to build the celebrated, but much more rider-friendly, Crystal Beach *Comet* (today's *Comet* at The Great Escape in Lake George, New York).

The Traver Engineering Company sometimes worked with other individuals and firms to produce coasters, notably designer Fred Church and his business partner Thomas Prior. Prior & Church (P.&C.) produced some amazing coasters, and some P.&C. projects involving Traver were masterpieces, notably the *Bobs*-series coasters, characterized by heavily banked turns, twisting trackage, sudden drops, and "trailered," flanged-wheeled coaster trains—necessary for exceptionally acrobatic trackage. Often cited as the P.&C./Traver team's all-time masterpiece was the Riverview *Bobs*, the Chicago park's signature coaster from 1924 to 1967. Though small by today's standards—it was only 87 feet high—the ride delivered by the *Bobs* put it into the all-time top 10 finest roller coasters ever to exist.

Church designed a multitude of excellent non-*Bobs* coasters as well, his most well-known perhaps being the harrowing *Aero-Coaster* at Playland Park in Rye, New York. Unfortunately, it was dismantled in 1957 due to low ridership—the ride was too terrifying for most park patrons! A more successful coaster—one of Church's best—was the *Cyclone Racer*, a landmark at The Pike in Long Beach, California, from 1930 to 1968. Three Church rides still operate: the wonderful *Dragon Coaster* at Playland Park near New York City, the *Giant Dipper* at Santa Cruz (California) Beach Boardwalk, and the stunningly restored *Giant Dipper* at Belmont Park in San Diego.

THE RISE, FALL, AND RISE OF COASTERS

Just as the popularity of amusement parks and their coasters pinnacled, the Great Depression reversed fortunes nationwide. For most U.S. parks and coasters, the Depression was akin to mass suicide, for an alarming number of parks and coasters were leveled. A post-Depression resurgence of parks and coasters was hampered by World War II, and although parks and coasters enjoyed a comeback during the postwar euphoria that swept the nation, another specter loomed: television.

TV entertainment was the new wonder of the 1950s and a strong contender for an evening summer stroll to Coney Island, Riverview Park, or wherever. A major recession in the late 1950s further stifled park (and therefore, coaster) growth—as did the increased public perception that amusement parks had become disreputable places (some had). As the 1960s played out, the downward spiral of parks accelerated, culminating in the destruction of some of the last great classic parks and coasters. Chicago's Riverview Park and its seven coasters closed suddenly at the end of the 1967 season; in 1968, California's extraordinary *Cyclone Racer* met an untimely demise when "developers" sought a permanent mooring for the retired ocean liner *Queen Mary*—they chose the *Racer's* pier; Euclid Beach in Cleveland succumbed in 1969; and the park of song and lore, Palisades Park in New Jersey, was leveled in 1972.

Fortunately, there were some silver linings. Riverview had debuted its "100 mile-per-hour" *Fireball* (actual top speed, about 50 m.p.h.) in 1963, and in 1965 opened its new *Jetstream* coaster. Also in 1965, Denver's Elitch Gardens

NEXT

The coaster renaissance that began in the 1970s can be traced to the opening of Kings Island's *Racer* in April 1972. Designed by the late John Allen, the *Racer* had a classic profile that provided a stunning backdrop to the Coney Island section of the new (1971) theme park. As of 1998, Kings Island had no fewer than seven coasters, but the *Racer* remains as well liked as ever. *Mike Schafer*

Following the introduction of the tubular steel-track coaster in 1959 came the first "inversion" coaster (a coaster with an upside-down element) since the turn of the century. Among the first of the species was the "corkscrew"-format coaster, most closely associated with the Arrow Development Company (now Arrow Dynamics). Northern Ohio's Geauga Lake was one of a legion of parks that ordered the radical new ride, shown barrel-rolling riders in 1980 as Geauga's more-traditional *Big Dipper* looms in the background. Compact rides with a short ride duration, the early corkscrews tend to have brief "shelf lives," and Geauga dismantled theirs after the 1997 season. *Mike Schafer*

revised its year-old *Mister Twister* coaster into what was destined to become a coaster legend during the approaching coaster renaissance. In 1968, Kennywood Park, near Pittsburgh, opened another legend-to-be, the *Thunderbolt*.

But another silver lining had particularly important, far-reaching effects on the future of roller coasters: the much-heralded 1955 opening of Disneyland in Anaheim, California. Though Disneyland never has been closely

associated with roller coasters (at the time of its opening, the new park didn't have any), Disneyland did popularize the controlled-access, theme-park concept—the key to the re-emergence of amusement parks and coasters.

The theme-park concept finally gained momentum in the 1970s, coinciding with a coaster renaissance that can be traced specifically to one park and one coaster. On April 29, 1972, the new Ohio-based Kings Island theme park, which had replaced Cincinnati's wonderful but flood-prone Coney Island park, debuted its brand-new giant wooden roller coaster, the twin-track *Racer*. The *Racer* was an architectural masterpiece with double the excitement. At nearly 90 feet high and with more than 3,400 feet of track on each circuit (the *Racer* is actually two mirror-image coasters) riding on dazzling white wood structure, the coaster was its own public relations statement. And the public was captivated.

Not only was the *Racer* stunning to behold, it was a delight to ride, by hard-core coaster buffs and family members of all ages alike. Immensely successful, the *Racer* had mass appeal and good looks that caught attention from coast to coast. Theme parks began to mushroom, and with them, new roller coasters. Further, surviving older parks also were affected by the theme-park-and-coaster craze, and they began to enjoy a resurgence.

The *Racer* was the brainchild of P.T.C. president and designer John Allen, who jettisoned to stardom as the man who almost single-handedly launched the coaster-building boom that continues to this day. Born in 1907, Allen went to work for P.T.C. in the 1930s, where he remained until his death in 1979. During his tenure, Allen designed numerous coasters and contributed immensely to coaster technology. The ride for which he is most-remembered was the unparalleled [*Mister*] *Twister* at the now-closed original Elitch Gardens site in Denver.

The new coaster renaissance ushered in other coaster designers who would make their marks in coasterdom: William Cobb, Charles Dinn, Anton Schwarzkopf, Michael Boodley, and others. Meanwhile, P.T.C. found itself facing a new legion of coaster-building companies, including Intamin, Curtis D. Summers Inc., and Arrow Development Company.

Arrow deserves a special mention, for it was Arrow, in conjunction with WED (Walter Elias Disney) Enterprises, that introduced breakthrough technology to coaster construction. Rewind back to 1959 when Disneyland was basking in unrivaled popularity and growth. That year, the park opened its *Matterhorn Bobsled* coaster—the first to employ lightweight coaster cars equipped with nylon wheels which gripped tubular-steel rails from three sides. The *Matterhorn* paved the way for a whole new generation of scenic railways, and during the 1960s, a number of "runaway mine train"-type coasters utilizing tubular steel-track technology began appearing at parks.

This new technology demanded close tolerances, but that in turn allowed for greater flexibility in track arrangement. In short, tubular track could almost literally be tied in giant knots, yet coaster trains could flow smoothly through the contortions. Why, the technology would even allow coasters to loop upside down . . .

And so they did. As the 1960s drew to a close and traditional parks and coasters were vanishing at an alarming rate, Arrow was experimenting with a "corkscrew" coaster which turned riders upside down for the first time since the early loopers at Coney Island. The first corkscrew coaster opened to the public in 1975 at Knott's Berry Farm, and the rest, as the old saying goes, is pretty much history.

True (vertical) loops followed, and soon tubular steel-track coasters established a whole new venue of rides that today dominates new coaster construction. These high-tech cousins to the traditional wood-track coaster deliver an entirely different type of ride, yet nicely complement their long-established wood brethren. From the looping coasters of the 1970s evolved still more amazing coaster varieties: the stand-up coaster, suspended coasters, inverted coasters, and others.

Despite the radical innovations spurred by the tubular-track technology, the traditional wood-track roller coaster endures, and indeed, thrives, remaining a favorite of veteran coasterholics as well as a whole new generation of riders. Although steel coasters now outnumber woodies, new wood coasters are still being built, for the wood coaster offers a ride experience—a kind of controlled recklessness, full of noisy abandon—that simply can't be duplicated by new technology. Nor would anyone want to. But together, steel- and wood-track coasters entice more riders than ever into the world of roller coasters, whose history has been full of ups and downs—and is now very "up."

2

Roller Coasters

of the
NORTHEAST

When the roller coaster immigrated to America, it landed in the historic Northeast. New York City's Coney Island became the germinating ground for the amusement park and the roller coaster in the 1800s, and both spread from there throughout America. Today, the world-renowned Coney Island *Cyclone* stands as a wild monument to those humble, quiet beginnings. During the Golden Age of parks and coasters—the early twentieth century—the Northeast in general became home to more parks and coasters than any other region in the country, and still offers some of the best coastering in America at some of the most memorable parks. A word of advice for those sampling Northeast coasters: start at Coney Island with the *Cyclone*—the coaster against which all others, in this and all other regions, are judged.

The incomparable *Thunderbolt* at Kennywood Park near Pittsburgh glows on a summer evening in 1980. Visible is the coaster's above-ground section, erected in 1968 and integrated with the 1920s-era *Pippin* coaster's "gully" section, hidden away at left out of the photo. The resulting new ride remained virtually unnoticed until the *New York Times* listed the *Thunderbolt* as No. 1 in a top 10 list. Despite dozens of newer, larger, and wilder coasters having been built since— including at Kennywood—the *Thunderbolt* remains one of the greatest roller coasters of the twentieth century. *Mike Schafer*

Workers rush to complete the *Riverside Cyclone* at Riverside Park near Springfield, Massachusetts, in early summer, 1983. Perilously angled track is a hallmark of the ride, which opened later in the 1983 season and became an instant hit among coaster fans. *Mike Schafer*

CONNECTICUT
Lake Compounce, Bristol (near Hartford)

Wildcat (1927)—*wood-track twister, 85 feet high, 2,746 foot run:* With its low-profile hills and track that swoops along undulating terrain, the *Wildcat* has long been known for high speed and good negative Gs. Completely rebuilt in 1986.

MAINE
Funtown USA, Saco

Excalibur (1998)—*wood-track twister, 100 feet high, 2,700-foot run:* *Excalibur* was the first wood coaster built in Maine in 60 years, and it's a doozy. With an 82-foot first drop, *Excalibur* reaches speeds of 55 mph while flying through drop curves,

over camel-backs, and through banked turns and an interesting figure-eight element.

MARYLAND
Adventure World, Largo (between Baltimore and Washington)

Mind Eraser (1995)—*steel-track inverted looper, 110 feet high, 2,172-foot run:* *Mind Eraser* riders board ski lift-like vehicles and embark on an intense tour of the convoluted steel trackage. Its extremely compact course contains five inversions.

Roar (1998)—*wood-track twister:* *Roar* is another ultra-twisted layout from the Golden Age-influenced imagination of coaster designer Michael Boodley/Great Coasters International. *Roar* combines all the best features of a well-orchestrated coaster:

The *Comet Flyer* at Whalom Park in Lunenburg, Massachusetts, shown in 1983, is a compact figure-eight/oval coaster that delivers an excellent ride; note the three layers of trackage on the left turnaround. The coaster now wears a new, lighter-colored paint scheme. *Mike Schafer*

stomach-gripping first drop, unpredictable directional changes, and unchecked speed.

Wild One (1917)—*wood-track out-and-back, 98 feet high, 4,000-foot run:* Known as the *Giant Coaster* when it stood at Paragon Park near Boston, this ride, with its snappy back turn, became a Marylander when it was moved to Wild World (now Adventure World) in 1986. An end-of-ride helix was added when the coaster was rebuilt at Wild World.

Jolly Roger Park, Ocean Park

Time Twister (1981)—*steel-track corkscrew, 75 feet high, 2,400-foot run:* The compact *Time Twister* takes its riders through swooping turns and a corkscrew element.

MASSACHUSETTS
Riverside Park, Agawam (near Springfield)

Mind Eraser (1997)—*steel-track inverted looper, 110 feet high, 2,172-foot run:* A near duplicate of the *Mind Eraser* at Maryland's Adventure World.

Riverside Cyclone (1983)—*wood-track twister, 107 feet high, 3,400-foot run:* You'll gasp as you peer down from the lift hill into the *Cyclone's* heavily banked first drop which turns and then catapults the train back up into a circle of track filled with lofty dips. The last half of the ride is relentless, with sudden, twisting drops, banked curves, and timbers flying by everywhere. Truly among the best of Northeast coasters!

Thunderbolt (1941)—*wood figure eight/oval, 70 feet high, 2,600-foot run:* Reportedly a favorite of the Kennedy family, the *Thunderbolt* provides a zesty ride that includes a double-dip, negative Gs, and a slide into home plate which leaves the underfriction wheels still spinning as riders detrain.

Whalom Park, Lunenburg

Comet Flyer (1940)—*wood oval/figure-eight, 65 feet high, 2,640-foot run:* From the man who brought you the fearsome Coney Island *Cyclone*—Vernon Keenan—comes this classic. This coaster packs a lot into a compact area, with excellent dips (reminiscent of 1920s-era coasters) that the whole family can enjoy.

NEW HAMPSHIRE
Canobie Lake, Salem

Canobie Corkscrew (1975)—*steel-track looper, 70 feet high, 1,250-foot run:* This coaster gets around in more ways than one. It first stood as *The Chicago Loop* at Chicago's now-defunct Old Chicago indoor amusement park. In 1981 it was moved to an Alabama park; Canobie acquired the ride in 1986-87.

Yankee Cannonball (1930)—*wood-track out-and-back, 64 feet high, 2,000-foot run:* This coaster is also a transplant, having originally stood at Waterbury, Connecticut; in 1933, it was moved to Canobie Lake. A good out-and-back coaster of the Golden Era.

NEW JERSEY
Clementon Lake Park, Clementon

Jack Rabbit (1919)—*wood oval/figure-eight, 50 feet high, 1,380-foot run:* One of the oldest operating coasters in America, the *Jack Rabbit* features a signature of its famous designer, John Miller: parabolic drops that go all the way to the ground.

Dinosaur Beach Pier, Wildwood

Crazy Mouse (1997)—*steel-track twister, 50 feet high, 1,377-foot run:* One of the new breed of *Wild Mouse*-style steel coasters sweeping the nation, *Crazy Mouse* has all the requisite hairpin turns and quick drops of its 1950s-era ancestor—but with tub-shaped cars that spin wildly!

Golden Nugget Mine Train (1960)—*steel-track scenic railway, 35 feet high, 900-foot run:* This unique coaster's trains encounter funhouse-like stunts along a layout that is partially enclosed. The only such coaster ever designed by P.T.C.

Morey's Pier, Wildwood

Great Nor'easter (1995)—*steel-track inverted looper, 115 feet high, 2,150-foot run:* Though similar to Adventure World's *Mind Eraser*, the *Great Nor'easter* is unique because it is built on a pier, *above* a water park, and it weaves tightly and sinuously around a log flume.

Wild Wheels Raceway & Adventure Pier, Wildwood

Great White (1996)—*wood-track twister with steel support, 110 feet high, 3,300-foot run:* The opening of this ride marked the return of wood-track coasters to the Jersey Shore—and it's a rollicking twister at that. *Great White* grabs you right from the start with a plunge into a dark tunnel that burrows beneath the pier toward the chain lift. The rest of the ride is a series of breathtaking drops, laterally banked turns, and air-time-filled rabbit hops.

Six Flags Great Adventure, Jackson

Batman—The Ride (1993)—*steel-track inverted looper, 105 feet high, 2,693-foot run:* A superb compact inverted coaster featuring five inversions.

Great American Scream Machine (1989)—*steel-track looper, 173 feet high, 3,800-foot run:* This powerful ride's element list includes three vertical loops, a boomerang, and a pair of corkscrews, all executed in dizzying succession.

Rolling Thunder (1979)—*wood-track out-and-back racer, 96 feet high, two 3,200-foot runs:* *Rolling Thunder* is very much two separate coasters in that, beyond a shared lift hill, each track circuit does its own thing. Ride both sides to see which you like best.

Viper (1995)—*steel-track "heartline" coaster, 88 feet high, 1,670-foot run:* A short, compact ride, *Viper* was the first U.S. installation of this radically new coaster breed. Riders experience steep drops and inversions that *rotate* the train. Prepare to spend some serious "hang time" during one of *Viper's* precarious rollovers.

NEW YORK
Astroland, Coney Island, Brooklyn

Cyclone (1927)—*wood-track twister with steel support, 85 feet high, 2,640-foot run:* Take to heart that you're riding the world's most famous roller coaster. With brute force, the renowned *Cyclone* will constantly remind you that it is Master of its Domain. Led off by an unusually steep (57 degrees) first drop, its tightly knit collection of wrenching turns and sudden plunges will make you think twice about that hot dog you just ate down the street at Nathan's. From the top of the *Cyclone's* lift hill, you can catch a glimpse of its moribund neighbor, the *Thunderbolt*, the famous *Wonder Wheel* Ferris wheel, and the Atlantic Ocean. After that, it's all a big blur.

The *Batman–The Ride* series of coasters appears at Six Flags parks in Illinois, California, and New Jersey. This 1993 view of *Batman* at Six Flags Great Adventure graphically illustrates the hellishly convoluted track layout shared by all the *Batmans*. *Terry Lind*

*R*olling *Thunder* at Six Flags Great Adventure is one of the most visually alluring coasters in the Northeast. As this view from the lift hill attests, each track of this racer has its own agenda, yet both trains manage to keep pace with each other if they are released from the station simultaneously. *Mike Schafer*

*B*rooklyn's tough guy: What the Coney Island *Cyclone* lacks in stature (it is "only" 85 feet tall) it massively makes up for in *chutzpah*. Its compact, twisted track plan walks on the wild side with its seemingly "straight down" first drop, high lateral forces on the tight turns, and sadistic, sudden dips that "spank" riders—nearly all of whom, of course, hurry back for more. *Both photos, Mike Schafer*

The celebrated *Blue Streak* at Conneaut Lake in Pennsylvania is a must-ride coaster in an intimate lakeside setting which includes a classic turn-of-the-century resort hotel. Imagine sitting on the peaceful, wide veranda of the Conneaut Lake Hotel one minute and in the lurching back seat of the *Blue Streak* the next—it's all possible at this great little park. *Mike Schafer*

The *Rollo Coaster* at Idlewild Park in Ligonier, Pennsylvania, is a "ridge runner," following the upper part of a small bluff at ground level (shown) before plunging into the valley. A nifty family ride at a newly rehabbed park. *Mike Schafer*

40

PENNSYLVANIA
Conneault Lake Park, Conneault Lake

Blue Streak (1937)—*wood-track out-and-back, 77 feet high, 2,900-foot run:* One of the best-loved old woodies still standing, the *Blue Streak* features a breathtaking first drop, especially for back-seat riders. It's not the length of the first drop; rather, it's the steepness and how the drop is partly obscured by trees. Back seat riders will feel as though they're going to be catapulted out of the train as it snaps over the lift hill. Beyond the speed bump at the bottom of the first drop are two classic camel-back hills, a speedy, banked turnaround, and a series of little camelback humps.

Dorney Park, Allentown

Hercules (1989)—*wood twister, 95 feet high, 4,000-foot run:* Don't let that 95-foot-high stat fool you—that's only how high the lift hill is above the coaster's main level. What you can't see from the boarding area is that the first drop plunges an awesome 148 feet over a bluff and into a vicious banked turn! After that, it's *uphill* back to the main level where the train dips and twists through its convoluted finale while the blood returns to the ashen faces of riders.

The *Sooperdooperlooper* at Hersheypark in Hershey, Pennsylvania, gets right down to business, heading into a vertical loop from the lift hill; then the track swoops through the center of the loop before heading into other portions of the park. *Mike Schafer*

For sheer, outrageous fun, Kennywood's *Racer* is about the best on the planet. Because this is a continuous, single-track racing coaster, the trains *must* race (on double-track racers, trains are not always released simultaneously, or one side may not be operating at all). This photo proves that it is possible to hold hands (albeit briefly) with the folks in the adjacent train. *Mike Schafer*

After San Antonio's *Rocket* was relocated from Texas to Pennsylvania and rechristened as the *Phoenix*, Knoebel's Grove park in Elysburg was suddenly thrust into coaster limelight. The *Phoenix*'s track crosses itself several times, figure-eight-style. Low-profile hills, as evident in this 1985 view from the first turnaround, are deceptively boisterous, and the ride as a whole is a speed demon. *Mike Schafer*

Lazer—*steel-track looper, 90 feet high, 2,200-foot run:* Imported from Brazil in 1986, this double-looper provides an exhilarating, swooping ride along a sensuous track profile.

Steel Force (1997)—*steel-track hypercoaster, 205 feet high, 5,600-foot run:* *Steel Force* is a ride to reckon with. It positively towers above everything in Dorney Park. A stomach-wrenching 205-foot, 60-degree plunge into a tunnel starts the action with a bang, and from there it never lets up. The 161-foot second hill is as good as the first, and the high-G spiraling turnaround will leave your head spinning. The spirited, rabbit-hop run back to the station is pure fun . . . but watch out for the double-up finale!

Thunderhawk (1924)—*wood-track out-and-back with a twist, 80 feet high, 2,767-foot run:* *Thunderhawk*'s slightly curved first drop sends the train racing along a speed-bump straightaway which then lofts it into a twisted knot of trackage that slams riders back and forth in their seats before the quick-dipping ride back to the station. Well into the 1980s, the *Thunderhawk* (then known simply as the Dorney *Coaster*) often made top 10 lists.

Hersheypark, Hershey (near Harrisburg)

Comet (1946)—*wood-track oval/out-and-back, 82 feet high, 3,360-foot run:* The handsome *Comet* is another longtime favorite of veteran coaster fans. The first drop over a pond is followed by a surprisingly narrow turnaround and another drop over the water. Following a thundering curve over the station (thereby heightening the anticipation of waiting riders below), *Comet* trains make a side trip to the Back 40 before returning home. A great way to cool off during a sultry Pennsylvania summer evening!

Sooperdooperlooper (1977)—*steel-track looper, 70 feet high, 2,614-foot run:* Though hardly intense by today's standards, *Sooperdooperlooper* is an enjoyable ride. The coaster gets right down to business with its vertical loop, and afterward the track swoops, dives, and circles around terrain, other rides, and itself.

The Great Bear (1998)—*steel-track inverted, 90 feet high, 2,800-foot run:* This $13 million constellation-themed ride sports smoothness and expert engineering. *The Great Bear* begins its trip atop a hill, drops 124 feet, and flies over the *Sooperdooperlooper.* From there the trains intertwine with other attractions and negotiate four inversions.

Trail Blazer (1974)—*steel-track "scenic railway," 43 feet high, 1,874-foot run:* Themed for the coal mines which populate eastern Pennsylvania, this short-but-sweet ride includes a helix.

Wildcat (1997)—*wood-track twister:* The *Wildcat* is a return to the rollicking wooden rides of the 1920s. Designer Michael

Boodley incorporated an astounding collection of heavily banked drops, turns, twists, and rabbit hops into the *Wildcat's* convoluted layout. Hersheypark did a magnificent job of lining the entire ride's course in bright white chase lights. This beautiful ride signals the rebirth of Golden Age-style twisters.

Idlewild Park, Ligonier (on the Lincoln Highway)

Rollo Coaster (1938)—*wood out-and-back, 27 feet high, 900-foot run:* Don't overlook this coaster because of its diminutive proportions—it's a gem! And *Rollo* is yet another example of the ravine coasters indigenous to Pennsylvania. After the first drop, the track rides along the ground at the top of a small bluff and then makes a punchy curved plunge down into the valley.

Wild Mouse (1988)—*steel-track twister, 60 feet high, 1,640-foot run:* An unusually large *Wild Mouse* entry from manufacturer Vekoma, this ride was originally located in England and came to Pennsylvania in 1993. The layout contains numerous zig-zags, hairpin turns, and abrupt drops.

Kennywood Park, West Mifflin (near Pittsburgh)

Jack Rabbit (1920)—*wood-track oval, 40 feet high, 2,132-foot run:* One of the most delightful coasters around, the *Jack Rabbit* operates much the same as it has for the last 75-plus years. The ride even retains its period-style trains, and the loading station with its neon jack rabbits is a classic. The *Jack Rabbit* is a ravine coaster in the best sense (as are all the Kennywood coasters), and its 70-foot double-dip off the lift hill is unparalleled. Hang on!

Racer (1927)—*wood-track racer, 76 feet high, 4,800-foot run:* Another Kennywood winner, the *Racer* is the only continuous-circuit, single-track racing coaster in America, so to cover its entire 4,800-foot run, you have to ride twice, making certain on your second trip that you board *from the side of the platform you last detrained from.* There's nary a straight track anywhere on the ride, so the *Racer* can be surprisingly disorienting, especially at night.

Steel Phantom (1991)—*steel-track twister/looper, 160 feet high, 3,000-foot run:* As if 160 feet weren't high enough, the *second* drop on this coaster is an astonishing 225 feet—right over the high bluff upon which Kennywood is perched. In fact, the *Steel Phantom* track slices through the *Thunderbolt*'s wooden structurework just before it swoops back up into a mind-numbing series of inversions.

Thunderbolt (1924/1968)—*wood out-and-back/ twister, 70 feet high, 2,887-foot run:* Consistently rated as one of the best coasters in the country (and for a time the No. 1 coaster on the

The first drop of Kennywood's *Steel Phantom* mimics that of the Crystal Beach *Cyclone* (1927–1947) by performing an almost vertical downward swoop. *Steel Phantom* towers over everything else in the park, even the world-class *Thunderbolt* (background), which *Phantom* goes *under*. Terry Lind

New York Times' best coaster list), the *Thunderbolt* continues to garner all sorts of superlatives from its riders and proves that size isn't everything. It began life as the *Pippin*, an out-and-back coaster built partly in a deep ravine. In 1968, Kennywood's Andrew Vettel replaced most of the *Pippin's* upper-level portion with a newly designed double swirl of banked trackage that brilliantly unites with the old ravine section. The unique combination of old and new results in a wonderfully disorienting ride—in classic, heavy-duty N.A.D. trains—whose *final* drop is, at some 90 feet, the longest on the ride.

Knoebel's Grove, Elysburg (near Shamokin)

Phoenix (1947)—*wood-track figure-eight, 78 feet high, 2,300-foot run:* One of the first wood coasters in recent times to be relocated, the *Phoenix* originally stood as the *Rocket* in San Antonio, Texas. Reassembled at Dick Knoebel's family-owned picnic grove park, the renamed ride—like its mythical namesake—acquired new life. And what a life! The *Phoenix* has become a favorite of "coasterholics," delivering a rip-snortin' ride during which trains scream around the circuit trying to tear themselves from the tracks.

Whirlwind (1984)—*steel-track looper, 64 feet high, 1,200-foot run:* The *Whirlwind* takes riders down a swooping first drop and through two corkscrews. It originally stood at Playland Park (Rye, New York) until 1992.

Lakemont Park, Altoona

Leap-the-Dips (1894)—*wood-track figure-eight:* As this book was being prepared, this coaster was undergoing restoration, and a reopening date was unknown. Whether running or not, *Leap-the-Dips* is worth checking out. This is the last surviving example of the once-common, turn-of-the-century figure-eight side-friction coaster in the U.S. If it reopens, *Leap-the-Dips* will regain its title of being the oldest operating roller coaster in North America.

Skyliner (1960)—*wood-track out-and-back, 60 feet high, 2,400-foot run:* An excellent family coaster, the *Skyliner* originally stood at Canandaigua, New York. Lakemont acquired the coaster in 1985 and reopened it in 1987. *Skyliner* still delivers a limber ride with its "folded water wing" track plan.

Waldameer Park, Erie

Comet (1951)—*wood-track oval/figure-eight, 45 feet high, 1,400-foot run:* Often called a "junior woodie" because of its modest proportions, the *Comet* is an ideal "beginner" ride for fledgling pre-teen coaster enthusiasts.

Williams Grove, Mechanicsburg (near Harrisburg)

Cyclone (1933)—*wood-track out-and-back, 65 feet high, 2,300-foot run:* This is a one-of-a-kind coaster in that it is double decked: the return run is directly below the outbound track run. The coaster trains are from the famous Palisades Park (New Jersey) *Cyclone*. An interesting ride in a funky little park!

3

Roller Coasters
of the
SOUTHLAND

Wild rides are hardly syn-
onymous with the congen-
ial, laid-back personality associated with America's Southern states. But
beyond those forested Appalachians, breezy palm
trees, and wide open Texas prairie lands await some
great coaster rides, both new and old. Besides, in the
South you'll find a longer—in some places year-
round—ride season, thus affording chilly Northerners
welcome relief from a January landscape of shuttered,
snow-covered coasters. Until the coaster boom of the
1970s, this region had suffered some serious coaster
extinction. Three notable survivors included the *Rocket*
in Norfolk, Virginia; the *Comet* at the Texas State
Fairgrounds near Dallas; and New Orleans' splendid
Zephyr coaster at Lake Pontchartrain, Louisiana. Alas,
the *Rocket, Comet,* and *Zephyr* succumbed in the early
1980s, but their spirits live on in a whole new family of
coasters that call the South "home."

Sun, surf, and coasters await coasterholics in search
of relief from less-hospitable climates. At the
Miracle Strip in Panama City, Florida, it's a hard choice
as to which is more inviting—the white sands and Gulf
waters or the *Starliner* roller coaster looming on the distant midway. Why not do both?! *Otto P. Dobnick*

47

This view of *Montu* riders graphically illustrates the meaning of "inversion" when it comes to roller coasters. The ride is the centerpiece of the new Egyptian section at Busch Gardens in Tampa, Florida. *Busch Gardens*

ALABAMA
Visionland, Bessemer

Rampage (1998)—*wood-track twister, 120 feet high, 3,500-foot run:* The brand new *Rampage* is a convoluted twister designed to tantalize riders with thrilling drops, wicked turns, and plenty of air time.

Waterville USA, Gulf Shore

Cannonball (1995)—*wood-track out-and-back, 65 feet high, 1,600-foot run:* This spirited coaster is packed with impressive air time and a speedy turnaround. Once again, a ride of the *Cannonball's* caliber proves that bigger is hardly ever better.

FLORIDA
Miracle Strip, Panama City

Starliner (1963)—*wood-track out-and-back, 70 feet high, 2,640-foot run:* This is another wonderful example of the late designer John Allen's smooth, no-nonsense work. The *Starliner* features a charming curved loading platform and numerous hills (many offering decent air time).

Tampa Bay Busch Gardens, Tampa

Kumba (1993)—*steel-track looper, 143 feet high, 3,978-foot run:* This sprawling thriller was the first "sit-down" coaster designed by the renowned Swiss firm of Bollinger & Mabillard. With passengers

Tunnels have been a part of coastering since the *Scenic Railway* days of the nineteenth century, and they're still a popular ride element. Miracle Strip's *Starliner* features a surprise, mid-course dragon-theme tunnel—complete with teeth. Campy, but effective! *Otto P. Dobnick*

Big Thunder Mountain Railroad is perhaps the ultimate modern scenic railway, complete with bat caves, avalanches, and other special effects that are a hallmark of in-house-designed Disney rides. In this 1996 scene on the railroad at Florida's Walt Disney World, one of the trains—complete with locomotive—rushes through the geyser section of the ride. *David P. Oroszi*

sitting four-abreast in eight-car trains, *Kumba* smoothly flies through seven inversions.

Montu (1996)—*steel-track inverted looper, 138 feet high, 3,983-foot run:* This bird-god-themed coaster executes its enormous elements with exceptional precision and grace. Like *Kumba*, riders sit four abreast, but the track is above their heads. From the pit of live crocodiles near the loading platform, to the "excavation" trenches and tunnel through which the trains dive and loop, you'll be completely amazed with *Montu*.

Python (1977)—*steel-track corkscrew, 70 feet high, 1,250-foot run:* This ride is similar to the Arrow-built *Corkscrews* operating at several other U.S. parks.

Scorpion (1980)—*steel-track looper, 65 feet high, 1,805-foot run:* Trains encounter a single vertical loop and heavily-banked spirals along the figure-eight course of this looping "speedracer."

Walt Disney World, Lake Buena Vista (Orlando area)

Big Thunder Mountain Railroad (1980)—*steel-track scenic railway, 2,780-foot run:* The runaway mine train format taken to the extreme. Five trains operate continuously along the multi-level track layout. Special effects include an avalanche, a bat cave, and an earthquake.

Gadgets Go Coaster (1993)—*steel-track junior twister, 28 feet high, 679-foot run:* Consisting of gentle drops and spirals, this steel coaster is of a new breed of rides aimed at younger children.

The *Dahlonega Mine Train* was the first coaster at Six Flags Over Georgia, and it remains one of the best mine-train-themed coasters. This 1986 scene shows one of the ride's, three lifts (background) and one of its longer tunnels. *Otto P. Dobnick*

The spirited *Cannon Ball* at Lake Winnepesaukah near Chattanooga, Tennessee, is a textbook example of an out-and-back coaster. The speed bumps between the two main hills on the outbound run and the numerous low-profile hills on the return will have you out of your seat as much as in it. *Mike Schafer*

Space Mountain (1975)—*steel-track twister, 90 feet high, Alpha track: 3,186-foot run/Omega track: 3,196-foot run:* This impressive ride is actually two separate coasters housed within a massive cone-shaped building. The two track layouts consist of tightly configured drops and spirals all executed within planetarium-like darkness. The sense of speed is greatly enhanced by the use of light and other special effects.

GEORGIA
Lake Winnepesaukah, Rossville (near Chattanooga, Tennessee)

Cannon Ball (1967)—*wood-track out-and-back, 70 feet high, 2,272-foot run:* The *Cannon Ball*'s trains—painted blue and gray in keeping with the Civil War theme—take a punchy ride over a traditional out-and-back circuit.

Riders of the *Great American Scream Machine* at Atlanta's Six Flags Over Georgia are treated to this stunning view of the coaster as the train creaks over the lift hill. With its white paint and red-and-blue trim, the *Scream Machine* is an all-American coaster ride and one of designer John Allen's best out-and-backs.

Six Flags Over Georgia, Atlanta

Batman–The Ride (1997)—*steel-track inverted, 100 feet high, 2,700-foot run*: Similar to *Batmans* at other Six Flags parks; see ride description for *Batman* at New Jersey's Great Adventure, Chapter 2.

Dahlonega Mine Train (1967)—*steel-track scenic railway, 37 feet high, 2,323-foot run*: Good tunnels and excellent landscaping make the *Dahlonega Mine Train* one of the better contemporary scenic-railway coaster rides.

Georgia Cyclone (1990)—*wood-track twister, 95 feet high, 2,970-foot run*: This was the second ride patterned after the world-famous Coney Island *Cyclone*, and many enthusiasts consider it the best of the lot. This *Cyclone* features a wonderful collection of steep drops, rambunctious turns, and lots of out-of-your-seat air time. Modern woodies don't get much better than this.

Great American Scream Machine (1973)—*wood-track out-and-back, 105 feet high, 3,800-foot run*: This was one of the earliest—and largest—woodies built during the early years of the roller coaster renaissance. The visually stunning *Great American Scream Machine* is another John Allen masterpiece.

Mind Bender (1978)—*steel-track twister, 97 feet high, 3,253-foot run*: Designer Anton Schwarzkopf's signature is swooping, sensuous track configurations, and perhaps that's what makes the *Mind Bender* a perennial favorite of coaster fans. You're riding a great coaster here, not a NASA stress test. *Mind Bender's* two vertical loops are exhilarating as is its unusual enter-from-the-top loop.

Ninja (1989)—*steel-track looper, 110 feet high, 2,900-foot run*: A compact coaster situated over a lagoon, *Ninja* features no less than five inversions. *Ninja* operated as *Kamikaze* at Wildwood, New Jersey, through 1991.

KENTUCKY
Kentucky Kingdom, Louisville

Chang (1997)—*steel-track stand-up looper, 154 feet high, 4,155-foot run*: When it debuted, *Chang* was the world's biggest stand-up coaster (it passed that honor to Six Flags Magic Mountain's *Riddler's Revenge* in 1998). This powerful, smooth ride turns passengers upside down five times.

Even youngsters can go coastering at Kentucky Kingdom—by climbing into the jumbo "roller skates" that serve as trains on the *Roller Skater*. *Terry Lind*

Roller Skater (1994)—*steel-track junior coaster, 28 feet high, 679-foot run:* A colorful and convoluted twister for kids. Each coach in the train is cleverly shaped like a giant roller skate.

Thunder Run (1990)—*wood-track twister, 88 feet high, 2,850-foot run:* Once your train drops down the first hill and into the brutally banked (at 80 degrees) curve, you'll realize this is an intense coaster! More tight turns follow, along with low-profile humps full of negative Gs.

Twisted Sister (1998)—*wood-track double coaster with steel support, 72 feet high, 2,640-foot run, each track:* This unusual double-tracked coaster is not a racer but designed so that the trains pass each other in opposite directions at high speeds. Highlights include perceived near misses and high-speed turns.

T² (Terror to the Second Power) (1995)—*steel-track inverted, 98 feet high, 2,172-foot run:* Essentially the same ride as the *Great Nor'easter* on Morey's Pier, Wildwood, New Jersey.

Kentucky Kingdom's *Thunder Run* brought wooden roller coasters back to Kentucky for the first time in many a moon. Trains roll off the lift-hill turnaround and drop into an unforgettable turn banked at 80 degrees (foreground). *Thunder Run* employs four-seat cars rather than the usual six-seaters so that trains may better negotiate the tight trackage. *Terry Lind*

54

Red Devil dispenses with the obligatory start-of-the-ride lift hill and gets right down to business by dropping riders 88 feet down a mountainside. With its lofty location high in North Carolina's Smoky Mountains, the *Red Devil*—and Ghost Town in the Sky in general—has one of the nicest settings of any coaster anywhere. *Otto P. Dobnick*

NORTH CAROLINA
Ghost Town in the Sky, Maggie Valley

Red Devil (1988)—*steel-track looper, 88 feet high, 2,037-foot run:* Perched atop one of the highest peaks in the Great Smoky Mountains, this unusual coaster begins with an 88-foot plunge directly off the loading into a single, high-G vertical loop and a series of spirals. A 90-foot chain lift brings the train back up the mountainside to the station.

Paramount's Carowinds, Charlotte

Carolina Cyclone (1980)—*steel-track looper, 95 feet high, 2,100-foot run:* The *Cyclone's* highlights include two vertical loops, two corkscrews, and a tunneled helix.

Gold Rusher (1972)—*steel-track scenic railway, 43 feet high, 2,397-foot run:* Carowinds' first coaster, this mine train contains two lifts, two quick spirals, and a surprise drop into a dark mine shaft. *Gold Rusher* is believed to be the first coaster to cross a state line, for its trains travel through a portion of South Carolina.

Hurler (1994)—*wood-track out-and-back, 83 feet high, 3,157-foot run:* Hurler's layout is identical to Kings Dominion's *Hurler*, with both opening the same year as centerpieces of new *Wayne's World*-themed areas. The course consists of one major hill and a succession of heavily banked, low-lying turns and rabbit hops. Air time? Abundant!

Scooby's Ghoster Coaster (1975)—*wood-track junior oval/figure-eight, 35 feet high, 1,385-foot run:* A sister to the junior coasters at Kings Island, Kings Dominion, and Canada's Wonderland.

The *Swamp Fox* had been a favorite at Myrtle Beach in South Carolina for nearly 25 years when suddenly, in 1990, it faced an uncertain future. But, the John Allen classic was resuscitated in 1992 to once again reign supreme along the Grand Strand. *Swamp Fox* has a lofty turnaround off the lift hill before the first drop, shown in this 1984 view. The second hill and one of the return hills are built above the brake run. *Otto P. Dobnick*

Who would have thought that the "I'm gonna hurl!" line popularized by *Saturday Night Live*'s "Wayne's World" sketches would have inspired a coaster name? But the moniker on the front of this coaster train hurtling along on Carowinds' *Hurler* proves that animals aren't the only things new coasters are named for. *Scott Rutherford*

Flanged wheels give all four consistently superior tracking and a smooth ride.

Thunder Road (1976)—*wood-track out-and-back racer, 93 feet high, 3,819-foot run:* When this ride first opened, it utilized beautifully articulated rolling stock from Riverview Park's (Chicago) *Jetstream;* it now uses standard P.T.C. trains. *Thunder Road*'s layout is nearly identical to that of Kings Dominion's *Rebel Yell*. Like its little sister, the *Gold Rusher, Thunder Road* crosses into South Carolina.

Vortex (1992)—*steel-track stand-up, 90 feet high, 2,040-foot run:* Vortex trains encounter a swooping first drop, vertical loop, an upward helix, and a disorienting corkscrew.

Vying with the distant Houston skyline, *Texas Cyclone* commands the attention of park patrons at AstroWorld. The *Texas Cyclone* was the first "offspring" of its Brooklyn (New York) prototype. Compare this view with that of its parent in Chapter 2, and you'll see the family resemblance. *Otto P. Dobnick*

SOUTH CAROLINA
Family Kingdom, Myrtle Beach

Swamp Fox (1966)—*wood-track out-and-back, 72 feet high, 2,640-foot run:* The *Swamp Fox* is a favorite among coaster enthusiasts due to its smooth, speedy ride (with plenty of air time) and its appealing home on the beach. The ride—another John Allen classic—was completely rebuilt for the 1992 season.

Pavilion Amusement Park, Myrtle Beach

Corkscrew (1978)—*steel-track oval/corkscrew, 70 feet high, 1,250-foot run:* One of the first of the modern looping coasters, this ride was originally located at now-defunct Magic Harbor south of Myrtle Beach; it was moved to Pavilion in the early 1980s. The layout is identical to the *Corkscrew* at Tampa Bay Busch Gardens and elsewhere.

Wild Mouse (1998)—*steel-track twister:* Just like its 1950s-era predecessor of the same name, this new-version *Wild Mouse* sends mouse-shaped cars through a series of impossibly tight hairpin turns and abrupt, steep drops. A wonderful replica of a proven classic.

TENNESSEE
Libertyland, Memphis

It may be elderly—the ride opened in 1923—but the *Zippin' Pippin* at Libertyland in Memphis, Tennessee, is no slouch; then again, few Miller & Baker coasters were. This 1983 view (sans Elvis) of the *Pippin's* brake run shows National Amusement Devices (N.A.D.) trains which have since been supplanted by P.T.C. rolling stock. Pippin, which is a variety of apple, was a popular coaster name in the 1920s. *Otto P. Dobnick*

Revolution (1979)—*steel-track looper, 70 feet high, 1,565-foot run:* *Revolution* features a 65-foot drop followed by a single vertical loop and a double corkscrew—a sister to the *Steamin' Demon* at The Great Escape in New York.

Zippin' Pippin (1923)—*wood-track oval/out-and-back, 70 feet high, 2,865-foot run:* This traditional woodie—Tennessee's only wood coaster—was a favorite of Elvis Presley before his catapult to stardom, although he was recently seen riding it again. The ride's layout consists of two sizable drops and turns followed by an undulating out-and-back run.

*S*hock Wave at Six Flags Over Texas in Arlington has the dubious distinction of being able to cause some riders to momentarily black out during its intense double-loop segment. Like its cousin, the *Mind Bender* at Six Flags Over Georgia, *Shock Wave* features the box-track construction common to Anton Schwarzkopf-built rides, but *Shock Wave* is considerably more rambunctious. *Mike Schafer*

TEXAS
AstroWorld, Houston

Batman—The Escape (1987)—*steel-track stand-up, 90 feet high, 2,300-foot run:* This ride debuted as *Shockwave* at Magic Mountain (California) in 1987 and moved to Great Adventure (New Jersey) in 1990. AstroWorld opened it in 1993 with an elaborate Batman theme.

Excalibur (1972)—*steel-track scenic railway, 88 feet high, 2,274-foot run:* *Excalibur* is a cross between a runaway mine train ride and a regular coaster, as its height will attest.

Mayan Mindbender (1988)—*steel-track twister, 27 feet high, 1,250-foot run:* This compact coaster, with its tightly configured gentle drops and spirals, was known as the *Nightmare* when it opened at Canada's now-defunct Bob-Lo Island. When it migrated to AstroWorld in 1995, it was set within a seven-story pyramid.

Serpent (1969)—*steel-track junior scenic railway, 20 feet high, 810-foot run:* Like its cousin *Mini Mine Train* at Six Flags Over Texas, the *Serpent* is the perfect starter coaster for young guests.

Texas Cyclone (1976)—*wood-track twister, 92 feet high, 3,184-foot run:* Briefly during the 1970s, the famed Coney Island (New York) *Cyclone* faced an uncertain future, but a rescuer stood by at the ready—AstroWorld, which intended to move the *Cyclone* to Houston. As it turned out, the original *Cyclone* got a new lease on life in Brooklyn, and AstroWorld still wound up with a *Cyclone*—by building a replica of the Coney ride. As a result, a new legend was born—the fearsome *Texas Cyclone*. Larger than the original, the *Texas Cyclone* amplified the *terrors* of its prototype, instantly propelling the Texas version to coaster stardom. Although coaster fans lament that AstroWorld "tamed" the ride during the mid-1980s, the *Texas Cyclone* remains a masterpiece of thrills with its steep, perilous drops and vicious fan turns.

Taz's Texas Tornado (1986)—*steel-track looper, 112 feet high, 3,280-foot run:* Among many hard-core enthusiasts, this incredible monster is the undisputed king of German steel coasters. From 1986 until its purchase by AstroWorld in the late 1990s, it toured German fairs as the *Thriller*. The compact ride is made up of steep power dives, tight turns, and four unconventional loops, the first two being legendary: their five-plus positive-Gs causes riders to black out!

Viper (1981)—*steel-track looper, 82 feet high, 1,942 foot run:* Originally known as the *Jet Scream* when it opened at Six Flags St. Louis in 1981, it was moved to Houston in 1989. It features a swooping first drop, single vertical loop, and a figure-eight blend of spirals.

XLR-8 (1984) *steel-track suspended, 81 feet high, 4,000-foot run:* XLR-8 was one of the first successful suspended coasters. The ride fea-

tures two lifts and a graceful collection of swooping climbs and dives. There's something very relaxing about a spin aboard this ride— imagine a train of in-line hang gliders.

Six Flags Fiesta Texas, San Antonio

Joker's Revenge—*steel-track looper:* Themed to one of Batman's arch enemies, *Joker's Revenge* is a standard single-loop/corkscrew ride, but with a twist: both trains run backward.

Pied Piper (1992)—*steel-track junior twister, 28 feet high, 679-foot run:* Basically the same ride as the *Roller Skater* at Kentucky Kingdom.

Rattler (1992)—*wood-track twister, 180.6 feet high, 5,080-foot run:* Constructed partially atop a soaring limestone quarry wall, the *Rattler* is an incredibly beautiful ride. When this serpent was first unleashed in 1992, it held the world record for having the longest drop—166 feet. The twisted, over-the-edge plunge was considered by many enthusiasts to be the best first drop ever on a wooden coaster. Unfortunately, some thought it a bit too wild for the general public, and in 1994 the bottom was raised 42 feet, forever removing the *Rattler's* potent bite. The remainder of the ride consists of two additional drops off the cliff (one into a tunnel blasted through the rock) and an undulating three-level helix.

Roadrunner Express (1997)—*steel-track scenic railway, 73 feet high, 2,400-foot run:* This Roadrunner-themed coaster features two lifts and plenty of tight drops and swoops, including passes through the structure of the neighboring *Rattler*.

Sea World of Texas, San Antonio

Great White (1997)—*steel-track inverted looper, 108 feet high, 2,562-foot run:* The first roller coaster to be installed at a Sea World park, the *Great White* is a superb compact inverted coaster featuring five inversions.

NEXT

No need to tell anyone that Texas always does things in a big way, and that applies to Lone Star coasters, too. For example, the crowning coaster achievement for Six Flags Over Texas thus far is the *Texas Giant*—nearly a mile of coaster madness and turmoil! When unveiled in 1990, it was the tallest wooden coaster in the world. Its ghostly presence in this 1992 night scene imparts unspeakable horror to uninitiated riders. *Terry Lind*

Coaster Technology

WHAT MAKES COASTERS STOP?

Automobiles, buses, trucks, and railroad locomotives and cars are all equipped with brakes to bring them to a stop. But not coaster cars or trains. Once over the lift hill, you are free-wheeling. "I'd like to get off before the next hill, please!" Sorry, you're outta luck. On roller coasters, only certain track segments are equipped with brakes—not the cars or trains themselves. Near the end of a coaster's circuit, trains enter the "brake run" and stop. There are two principal types of braking systems. "Skid" brakes feature brake rails, located between the running rails, that are activated by a ride operator or computer. They raise, pushing against brake pads mounted under each coaster car to slow or stop the train. The second type is a "squeeze" brake. Brake bars squeeze—vise-grip-style—against brake fins mounted under or on the sides of each car. Coaster-braking systems are usually "fail safe." A power outage will result in spring mechanisms defaulting the brakes to "activate" mode. This 1985 view of the Clementon Lake (New Jersey) Jack Rabbit shows the brake run leading into the station. The brake bars can be seen between the running rails behind the train, which has just been unloaded. The train is about to be released to coast forward one train length, where another brake will stop it for boarding.

Six Flags Over Texas, Arlington (Dallas/Fort Worth)

Judge Roy Scream (1982) *wood-track out-and-back, 65 feet high, 2,670-foot run:* With its super smooth ride and intermediate-size hills, *Judge Roy Scream* is an ideal family coaster.

La Vibora (1984)—*steel-track bobsled, 60 feet high, 1,490-foot run:* Basically a duplicate of the *Lake Placid Bobsled* at New York's Great Escape.

Mini Mine Train (1969)—*steel-track junior mine train, 20 feet high, 710-foot run:* A pint-sized version of its big brother, *Run-A-Way Mine Train*, located next door.

Run-A-Way Mine Train (1966)—*steel-track scenic railway, 35 feet high, 2,400-foot run:* This historically significant attraction was the very first mine train-themed coaster, and it paved the way for a long list of similar rides. A relatively lengthy ride, it features three lifts, tight turns, and a surprise drop into a tunnel beneath a lake.

Shock Wave (1978)—*steel-track twister/looper, 116 feet high, 3,500-foot run:* This high-speed coaster is known for actually causing some riders (including one of this book's authors) to momentarily black out during the heavy G-force fling through the ride's double-loop section.

Texas Giant (1990)—*wood-track twister, 143 feet high, 4,920-foot run:* Widely considered to be coaster designer Curtis Summers' masterpiece and one of the world's top existing wood coasters, the *Texas Giant* is extreme coastering at its best. From a steep first drop to lightning-fast turns and drops and unpredictable directional changes, the *Texas Giant* will leave you gasping. And that's just the first two-thirds of the ride! The final 1,000 feet of track is pure genius: speeding trains drop *into* the structurework supporting the first high turns and begin a rapid series of twisting, turning speed bumps that make riders feel as if they're strapped onto a bucking bronco. The train leaps up into the brake run with so much unused energy that the entire brake shed trembles. There's nothing quite like the *Texas Giant*.

Wonderland Amusement Park, Amarillo

Texas Tornado (1985)—*steel-track looper, 80 feet high, 2,050-foot-run:* The *Tornado* is a short ride, but unusually intense. Two high-G vertical loops are among its highlights, as is the surprise plunge from the second loop into an underground tunnel.

VIRGINIA
Busch Gardens Old Country Williamsburg, Williamsburg

Alpengeist (1997)—*steel-track inverted looper, 195 feet high, 3,828-foot run:* *Alpengeist* is a marvel of modern engineering. Cleverly themed as an out-of-control ski lift, the ride is strategically

The *Avalanche* at Paramount's Kings Dominion near Richmond, Virginia, harkens to a short period during the first half of the twentieth century when trough-track coasters enjoyed popularity. Usually known as *Flying Turns* or carrying a moniker that included the word "bobsled," these coasters simulated a frightening scream down an icy bobsled track. The concept has returned to a number of parks. *Thomas Faw, Terry Lind Collection*

The interlocking vertical loops of *Loch Ness Monster* provide an entertaining centerpiece to Busch Gardens Williamsburg. The lower train in this scene has just come off the first lift hill while the second train, in the upper loop, is in the final throes of the circuit before returning to the station. *Otto P. Dobnick*

Hidden away at a classic little traditional amusement park on the outskirts of Huntington, West Virginia, is the *Big Dipper*, running much the way it always has for some 40 years. Vintage N.A.D. trains carry riders around a frisky figure-eight track route that ends up in a tunnel, visible just below the train in this 1991 view. *Mike Schafer*

placed among the forested ravines of beautiful Busch Gardens. To describe *Alpengeist* (think "Alpine poltergeist") as powerful would be an understatement; this snow beast grabs you from the beginning and refuses to let go until you hit the brakes at ride's end. Highlights include a 17-story swirling plunge into a valley and a power dive through a warming hut. Ghostly night rides on *Alpengeist* are unbelievable.

Big Bad Wolf (*1984*)—*steel-track suspended, 100 feet high, 2,800-foot run:* This highly regarded steelie is one of the few major coasters to feature two lift hills. The ride is themed a la "Little Red Riding Hood"; trains whip relentlessly through a forest and an "abandoned" German village besieged by wolves, finally plummeting into a river valley.

Drachen Fire (*1992*)—*steel-track looper, 150 feet high, 3,440-foot run:* A large looper, *Drachen Fire* begins with a shallow drop off the chain into a one-of-a-kind sweeping corkscrew, nearly 15 stories above the forest floor. From there, the trains encounter a rapid-fire succession of disorienting elements.

Loch Ness Monster (*1978*)—*steel-track looper, 130 feet high, 3,240-foot run:* Best-known for its steep first drop, this serpentine ride was one of the earliest major looping coasters. *Nessie's* signature element involves two intertwining vertical loops, through which trains loop simultaneously—a spectacular sight for bystanders as well as riders.

Wild Maus (*1996*)—*steel-track twister, 46 feet high, 1,217-foot run:* This ride debuted at Busch Gardens as *Wild Izzy* in honor of the Olympic Games and was slated to be dismantled at the end of the season, but it proved so popular, Busch Gardens kept *Izzy* in operation. It was one of the first new *Wild Mouse*-type rides and features all the typical hairpin turns and abrupt drops of that 1950s' U.S. classic.

Paramount's Kings Dominion, Doswell (Richmond)

Anaconda (*1991*)—*steel-track looper, 144 feet high, 2,700-foot run:* Built almost completely over water, this ride starts off with a suicidal banked plunge into a tunnel beneath the surface of a lake. From there, riders encounter a sidewinder, an unusual knot of track called a "butterfly," and a corkscrew finale.

Avalanche (1988)—*steel-trough track bobsled, 60 feet high, 1,906-foot run:* Avalanche is the closest any manufacturer has come to recreating the feel of the long-lost *Flying Turns* coasters of the Golden Age. Wherein those coasters employed a track trough usually made of cypress wood, the new version utilizes ribbed steel. And like an actual bobsled, the freewheeling trains negotiate surprise down slopes, S-curves, and severely banked turns.

Grizzly (1982)—*wood-track oval/twister, 87 feet high, 3,150-foot run:* This beast is a beauty! Patterned after the late, lamented *Wildcat* coaster that once reigned over Cincinnati's Coney Island, the *Grizzly* haunts a thickly wooded section of King's Dominion, delivering an excellent ride featuring fan turns, speed bumps, and curving plunges.

Hurler (1994)—*wood-track out-and-back, 83 feet high, 3,157-foot run:* Hurler is identical to the *Hurler* at Paramount's Carowinds (Charlotte, North Carolina).

Rebel Yell (1975)—*wood-track out-and-back racer, 86 feet high, two 3,368-foot runs:* Like a few other coasters, *Rebel Yell* is a Hollywood star, having appeared in the 1977 thriller *Rollercoaster*. The ride is a direct descendant and near duplicate of the coaster that ushered in the coaster boom of the 1970s, Kings Island's *Racer*.

Scooby Doo (1975)—*wood-track junior figure-eight/oval, nearly 35 feet high, 1,385-foot run:* The big kids at Kings Dominion got a swell new wood coaster in 1975 (previous entry), so it was only fair the little kids got one too. *Scooby Doo* delivers a spunky ride that's perfect for up-and-coming coaster fans. (And we've seen big kids enjoy it, too.)

Shockwave (1986)—*steel-track stand-up looper, 92 feet high, 2,231-foot run:* Shockwave passengers stand two-abreast to experience a vertical loop, speedy camelback, and a high-G-force downward spiral.

Volcano: The Blast Coaster (1998)—*linear-induction suspended coaster, 2,757-foot run:* Volcano is the world's first linear-induction suspended roller coaster. Its riders sit two-abreast in four-car trains and are propelled at 70 mph via electromagnetic energy into the heart of a "volcano." They then blast upside down out of the peak and negotiate heartline spins down through the mountain.

WEST VIRGINIA
Camden Park, Huntington

Big Dipper (1958)—*wood-track oval/figure-eight, 50 feet high, 1,800-foot run:* Though considered by some to be a "junior" coaster, this woodie has nothing to apologize for: it appeals to riders of all ages, with a double dip, tunnel, and vintage N.A.D. trains.

Lil' Dipper—*wood-track oval, steel support, 17 feet high, 450-foot run:* This is the only known surviving example of N.A.D.'s stock model "kiddie coaster." The trains are miniature versions of the N.A.D. trains on the nearby *Big Dipper*.

Roller Coasters

4

of the
HEARTLAND

America's Heartland has long been a bastion of amusement parks, thanks in part to the region's extensive network of interurban and trolley railway companies, which often developed parks to lure riders. Also, Midwesterners simply have always had a penchant for fairs, carnivals, and kindred forms of outdoor entertainment. The Midwest likewise has a rich coaster heritage, the nucleus of which was Chicago's legendary Riverview Park and its premier ride, the *Bobs*—a coaster which, to this day, is still spoken of in hushed tones of reverence by longtime coaster fans. Featuring as many as 11 coasters at one time, Riverview was the penultimate coaster park, and its surprise closing in 1967 left a coaster void that was only amplified by similar park closings elsewhere in the Midwest, notably Cleveland's Euclid Beach, St. Louis' Forest Park, and Cincinnati's Coney Island. But from the ashes of these coaster meccas arose new parks and coasters, while surviving old parks rushed new coasters into action.

Frontier City's *Wildcat* was a Kansas City (Missouri) star until its home, Fairyland Park, closed in 1977. The ride stood moribund for more than a dozen years before Oklahoma City's Frontier City, cheered on by coaster preservationists, not only resurrected the *Wildcat*, but added additional ride elements. With its unusual red-painted track and vintage N.A.D. trains, the *Wildcat* romps again. *Terry Lind*

ILLINOIS
Hillcrest Park, Romeoville (Chicagoland) NOTE: Home office is in Lake Zurich

Little Dipper (1952)—*wood-track figure-eight/oval, 24 feet high, 700-foot run:* A "catalog" P.T.C. "kiddie coaster," *Little Dipper* originally stood at another small Chicagoland park until relocated to Hillcrest circa 1967. This is a difficult coaster to ride, as the park caters only to private picnic parties. Round up all your friends and give Hillcrest a call.

Kiddieland, Melrose Park (Chicagoland)

Little Dipper (1950)—*wood-track figure-eight/oval, 24 feet high, 700-foot run:* Kiddieland immaculately maintains its *Little Dipper*, a twin to the Hillcrest ride (previous entry) in terms of track layout. It even features a neon LITTLE DIPPER sign.

Three Worlds of Santa's Village, East Dundee (Chicagoland)

Typhoon (1998)—*steel-track looper, 63 feet high, 1,836-foot run: Typhoon* is the first ride of its kind in the U.S. A diving first drop leads

Chicago's renaissance as a coaster haven took a great leap forward with the 1981 opening of the *American Eagle* at Great America. The view from the lift hill of the *American Eagle* is one of the greatest in all of coasterdom, thanks in part to the spectacular, lofty helix which awaits at the opposite end. The only thing separating you from the rest of the ride at this point is a 55-degree, 147-foot drop—one of the steepest on any wood-track coaster (about the same as the Coney Island *Cyclone*). *Mike Schafer*

the three-car train into an unusual tilted vertical loop and an upward spiral.

Six Flags Great America, Gurnee (northern Chicagoland)

American Eagle (1981)—*wood-track out-and-back racer, 127 feet high, 4,650-foot run:* This monster has become a landmark for motorists traveling between Chicago and Milwaukee on I-94. Like nearly all other racers, the *Eagle* is essentially two coasters; each track is independent of the other. The first

Introduced in 1988, Great America's *Shock Wave* was among the first of a whole new breed of mega-steelies to sweep the nation. The first drop, which twists as it descends, lofts the trains up into a vertical loop that's nearly in the stratosphere. Most of the ride's seven inversions are visible in this eastward view, which reveals that the coaster was actually erected in the parking lot. *Terry Lind*

drop is one of the best, and the swirl through the outer-end helix is energizing.

Batman–The Ride (*1992*) —*steel-track inverted looper, 100 feet high, 2,700-foot run:* This was the world's first inverted coaster and it paved the way for a whole new generation of steel coasters. Like all its same-name clones, *Batman's* riders sit in ski lift-like vehicles and experience two vertical loops, a zero-G roll, and a pair of corkscrews.

Demon (*1980*)—*steel-track looper, 82 feet high, 1,250-foot run:* This coaster began life in 1976 as the *Turn of the Century*. Originally it featured two hills which led to a corkscrew finale—at the time a revolutionary ride element. The ride went through a drastic rebuild in 1980 in which the hills were replaced by two vertical loops and heavy theming which included demonic sound effects and a strobe-lighted tunnel.

Iron Wolf (*1990*)—*steel-track stand-up looper, 100 feet high, 2,900-foot run:* With ultra-smooth trackwork and precise engineering, this stand-up ride was a preview of what the now-famous Swiss firm of Bollinger & Mabillard had up its sleeves. This ride sports twisting drops, a vertical loop, spirals and a corkscrew.

Shock Wave (*1988*)—*steel-track looper, 170 feet high, 3,900-foot run: Shock Wave* was the first of Six Flags' three mega-loopers, and many consider it the most powerful. At breakneck speed, riders zoom down a harrowing 155-foot twisting first drop and through three lofty vertical loops, a boomerang, and a pair of corkscrews.

Viper (*1995*)—*wood-track twister, 100 feet high, 3,458-foot run:* The *Viper* is the latest Six Flags woodie patterned after the Coney Island *Cyclone,* but Six Flags ride specialists took liberties with the design and added a few surprises of their own.

Whizzer (*1976*)—*steel-track twister, 70 feet high, 3,100-foot run:* The *Whizzer* is a big brother to the portable *Jet Star* and *Jumbo Jet* coasters found throughout the world and is unusual in several respects. Rather than the traditional chain system of hoisting trains up the lift hill, the trains themselves contain small traction motors which lift them, cog-railway-style, to the top. In addition, riders ride single file, straddling the seats. The two-minute ride includes several swooping, banked turns.

INDIANA
Indiana Beach, Monticello

Hoosier Hurricane (*1994*)—*wood-track out-and-back, steel support, 100 feet high, 3,000-foot run:* At a loss for space, Indiana Beach located the thrilling *Hoosier Hurricane* above existing attractions and out over Lake Shafer. The *Hurricane* features plenty of tall, steep drops, a swooping turnaround, and a good dose of air time on the run home.

70

The *Hoosier Hurricane* at Indiana Beach in Monticello, Indiana, proved an excellent addition to this gem of a park astride Lake Shafer; in fact, the *Hurricane* is in part built *over* the lake. Like only a few other wood-track coasters, the *Hurricane* utilizes steel support structure. *Terry Lind*

When the fledgling Adventureland in Des Moines, Iowa, decided to risk capital for a major woodie in the late 1970s, the result was the *Tornado*, designed by the late Bill Cobb who also designed the *Texas Cyclone*. Although initially a "no frills" intermediate-size coaster with but one train (it now has two) and manual brakes, the *Tornado* turned out to be a powerful ride. *Mike Schafer*

Holiday World, Santa Claus

The Raven (1995)—*wood-track twister, 110 feet high, 2,800-foot run:* Appropriately located in the park's Halloween section, *The Raven* is one wicked little ride. You really can't see much of its layout since it's hidden within a dense forest, and that's part of its charm. An 86-foot first drop dives into a tunnel and then swoops down for a peek at Lake Rudolph before climbing back up the hillside . . . and then the real fun begins. A surprisingly steep drop sends the train on a wild rampage through the woods, dodging trees and tossing riders like rag dolls (the air time on this ride is otherworldly!). Tip: night rides will blow you away as there are no lights on the circuit.

IOWA
Adventureland, Des Moines

Dragon (1990)—*steel-track looper, 90 feet high, 2,250-foot run:* Built partially over a lagoon, *Dragon* thrills riders with a series of choppy rabbit hops before the chain, a pair of back-to-back vertical loops, and a quick spiral.

Outlaw (1993)—*wood-track twister, 70 feet high, 2,600-foot run:* Designer Michael Boodley's trademark twisting turns and expert transitions are here in abundance. Despite its modest size, the *Outlaw* is a wonderfully entertaining woodie. A banked first drop, a wild S-turn, endless curves, and smooth tracking are highlights.

Tornado (1978)—*wood-track out-and-back, 93 feet high, 2,840-foot run:* Named for the weather phenomenon that ravished the park in 1974, this coaster storms through its paces. The nice first drop leads to a steep, curved ascent which slows the train considerably, lulling riders into thinking this is going to happen again on

Giant Coaster roams about Iowa's Arnolds Park and along Lake Okoboji, providing riders with plenty of John Miller camel-hump hills. The ancient two-car P.T.C. trains shown in this 1980 view have since been replaced with vintage, secondhand N.A.D. trains, following *Giant Coaster*'s revamping. *Mike Schafer*

Kansas' only woodie as this book goes to press is the cleverly named *Roller Coaster* at Wichita's Joyland Park. You get two trips for the price of one on this coaster: a cool ride on a doglegged out-and-back P.T.C. coaster as well as a "trip" back to the 1950s while you stroll into the coaster station. *Otto P. Dobnick*

The *Excaliber* coaster at Valleyfair! in Shakopee, Minnesota, is a departure from the norm, for it incorporates a combination of delicate-looking wood and steel structurework. But it's a real twister, with drops that nearly touch the ground, and the resulting appearance suggests a coaster that has partially collapsed but remains running! *Excalibur*'s first drop—at 60 degrees—vies with Cedar Point's *Magnum* as the steepest of any coaster. *Terry Lind*

subsequent crests. Wrong. There's no let-up beyond, and the turn-back curve packs a wallop you'll feel for the rest of the ride home.

Arnolds Park Amusement Park, Arnolds Park

Giant Coaster (1927) *wood-track oval, 63 feet high:* Heightwise, *Giant Coaster* isn't a giant, but it does have a giant footprint, circling the entire amusement park along Lake Okoboji, Iowa's most famous resort lake. The ride is textbook John Miller: its dips go all the way to the ground. *Giant Coaster* was closed in the mid-1980s, purchased by new owners, lovingly restored, and reopened in 1989, with "new" trains from defunct Mountain Park's *Flyer* at Holyoke, Massachusetts.

KANSAS
Joyland, Wichita

Roller Coaster (1949)—*wood-track out-and-back, 80 feet high, 2,600-foot run:* This baby boomer features a classic 1950s-era boarding station and intricately painted trains—original P.T.C. rolling stock, no less. The first drop swoops into a shallow valley shrouded by trees, and the track plan then follows a L-shape route, chock full o' humps.

MICHIGAN
Michigan's Adventure, Muskegon

Corkscrew (1979)—*steel- track corkscrew, 70 feet high, 1,250-foot run:* The *Corkscrew* is a "catalog" coaster purchased by a number of parks when the corkscrew format was a wild, new innovation.

Shivering Timbers (1998)—*wood-track out-and-back, 125 feet high, 5,200-foot run:* An enormous ride, *Shivering Timbers'* 125-foot first drop is followed by vertical plunges of 100, 80, and 50 feet. There is

very little slow-down over the crests, guaranteeing butterflies for everyone. The swooping turnaround positions the train for a rapid airtime-filled romp back to an upward helix before roaring into the brakes.

Wolverine Wildcat (1988)—*wood-track oval, 85 feet high, 3,000-foot run:* The spunky *Wolverine Wildcat* parrots the *Comet* at Lake George, New York, with high turnarounds connected by low-profile speed-bump runs.

Zach's Zoomer (1994)—*wood-track junior twister, 30 feet high, 2,000-foot run:* An impressive ride with numerous hills and speedy turnarounds, all gentle enough for young children. The ride is named after park owner Roger Jourden's grandson.

MINNESOTA
Knott's Camp Snoopy, Bloomington (suburban Twin Cities)

Ripsaw (1992)—*steel-track twister, 60 feet high, 2,680-foot run:* Ripsaw is the centerpiece of Mall of America's indoor Camp Snoopy and perfect for riders young and old. Built above the action on the ground, *Ripsaw* features two tire-driven lifts, shallow drops, and swooping turns.

Valleyfair!, Shakopee (near the Twin Cities)

Corkscrew (1980)—*steel-track corkscrew, 85 feet high, 1,950-foot run:* Once Arrow Dynamic's compact *Corkscrew* coaster of the mid-1970s had proven itself, expanded versions such as this became available with an extended track run and a vertical loop.

Excalibur (1989)—*steel-track twister, 117 feet high, 2,415-foot run: Excalibur* is a cousin of Cedar Point's *Gemini*—they share a trait of having tubular steel track on wooden structure. With a 60-degree first drop, this exciting coaster whips through a series of severely banked turns, drops, and quick direction changes.

High Roller (1976)—*wood-track out-and-back, 70 feet high, 2,982-foot run:* A coaster with classic camelback hills, *High Roller* also delivers some good negative Gs. It's also one of the few newer coasters to feature highly regarded, solid-riding N.A.D. cars.

Wild Thing (1996)—*steel-track hypercoaster, 200 feet high, 5,640-foot run:* Obviously inspired by Cedar Point's *Magnum XL-200, Wild Thing's* 196-foot first drop, angled at 60 degrees, is oh so sweet, and cranks the train's speed up to 74 mph. The 98-foot-tall second hill was designed to produce sustained low-Gs.

MISSOURI
Six Flags St. Louis, Eureka (near St. Louis)

Batman–The Ride (1995)—*steel-track inverted looper, 105 feet high, 2,693-foot run:* This *Batman* is identical to those operating at other Six Flags theme parks, except that its layout is a mirror image of its brothers.

Ninja (1986)—*steel-track twister, 110 feet high, 2,330-foot run: Ninja* emigrated from Expo '86, Vancouver, British Columbia. It proves that looks are deceiving. *Ninja's* numerous ride elements— loop, barrel rolls, spirals—are compacted such that the ride does not appear to be particularly threatening, but it's intense and quite disorienting. "That'll teach ya," it seems to say as you wobble down the exit ramp.

River King Mine Ride (1971)—*steel-track scenic railway, 2,349-foot run:* This ride began as an unusual twin-track mine train ride. One track was relocated to Dollywood park in Tennessee.

Screamin' Eagle (1976)—*wood-track out-and-back, 110 feet high, 3,872-foot run:* The *Screamin' Eagle* forms a magnificent backdrop to the park, located along a hillside. This was the last coaster to be designed by the late John Allen (and his favorite), who left his mark on many renaissance-era woodies. The *Screamin' Eagle's* long, smooth, L-shaped out-and-back run is rife with big, parabolic hills, the longest drop (92 feet) being the third—not the first.

Worlds of Fun, Kansas City

Mamba (1998)—*steel-track hypercoaster, 205 feet high, 5,600-foot run: Mamba* is the Midwest's tallest and fastest coaster. This towering ride's 205-foot first hill, angled at 60 degrees, is guaranteed to take your breath away, but so is the second: it drops 179 feet and propels the train again to the near-maximum velocity of 75 mph. A 580-degree high-G turnaround leads into a series of rabbit hops en route back to the station.

Orient Express (1980)—*steel-track twister/looper, 120 feet high, 3,470-foot run: Orient Express* is a smooth-running cousin to the *Loch Ness Monster* of Busch Gardens Williamsburg, right down to its two interlocking loops; in fact, the two rides share surprisingly similar stats. The main difference? *Orient Express* has a "boomerang" (see glossary).

Timber Wolf (1989)—*wood-track twister/out-and-back, 100 feet high, 4,230-foot run: Timber Wolf* turned out to be the "dark horse" award winner of new coasters in 1989, and it remains a favorite. *Timber Wolf* features eclectic track arrangements. One minute you're dropping down a traditional, breathtaking hill, and the next you're spiraling upward in a helix. The ride's relatively low-profile dips translate to breakneck speeds, lots of negative Gs, and banked turns.

OHIO
Americana Park, Middletown (near Cincinnati)

Screechin' Eagle (1927)—*wood-track out-and-back, 78 feet high, 2,640-foot run*: Screechin' Eagle is a punch-packing coaster from beginning to end. Typical of coasters created by the famed John Miller, most of its hills plunge all the way to ground level, and with considerable steepness. As a result, the *Screechin' Eagle* provides a raucous back seat ride: You'll swear it's gonna fling you out into the nearby lake.

Cedar Point, Sandusky

Blue Streak (1964)—*wood-track out-and-back, 78 feet high, 2,558-foot run*: Though a relative latecomer, the *Blue Streak* has an early twentieth century look to it, right down (or up) to the cuspate-roofed "cap" at the top of the lift hill.

Timber Wolf is an action-packed coaster that has put Kansas City, Missouri's Worlds of Fun park on the big-time coaster map. It stands at the edge of the park, its pure form (and fun) uninhibited by other rides and buildings. *Terry Lind*

Magnum, at Cedar Point in Sandusky, Ohio, gives new meaning to "astonishing height." Its 205-foot-high lift hill enables riders aboard trains equipped with oxygen masks to see Toledo, Cleveland, and maybe Detroit (well, not really, but this coaster *is* genuinely *high*). In this 1992 view from good 'ole Mother Earth, one train returns from its flight as another heads up, up, and away while riders learn the meaning of "acrophobia." *Terry Lind*

Painted in shades of blue, of course, the *Blue Streak* features flat (versus parabolic) ascents and descents, which add to the feeling that the train is going to launch itself from each peak.

Cedar Creek Mine Ride (1969)—*steel-track scenic railway,* 48 *feet high,* 2,540-*foot run:* A lagoon serves as the focal point to this runaway mine train ride, which is considered one of the best in its class.

Corkscrew (1976)—*steel-track corkscrew,* 85 *feet high,* 2,050-*foot run:* Similar to other intermediate-size Arrow corkscrews (e.g., at Minnesota's Valleyfair!), this ride enjoys prominence in the public eye: its corkscrew element flies right above one of the park's main walkways.

Disaster Transport (1985)—*steel-trough bobsled,* 63 *feet high,* 1,932-*foot run:* When opened in 1985, this was a standard bobsled coaster, named *Avalanche Run.* In 1990, Cedar Point enclosed the entire ride and gave it an outer space theme.

75

Gemini (1978)—*steel-track figure-eight/oval racer, 125 feet high, 3,935-foot run, each track:* One of the few steel-track racing coasters, *Gemini* is also unusual in that it has a wood support structure. Other *Gemini* claims to fame are its impressive 60-degree, 125-foot first drop and six high-capacity trains.

Iron Dragon (1987)—*steel-track suspended, 76 feet high, 2,800-foot run:* This two-lift ride is located partially on an island, and during its first half, the trains swoop gracefully among the treetops. After the second lift, riders are treated to a tight pretzel-like element over the waters of a foggy lagoon.

Junior Gemini (1979)—*steel-track kiddie coaster, 19 feet high, 443-foot run:* The perfect "starter" for those up-and-coming coaster fans. *Junior Gemini*'s trains even resemble those of its big brother, which looms nearby.

Magnum XL-200 (1989)—*steel-track hypercoaster, 205 feet high, 5,106-foot run:* *Magnum,* a non-looping steel coaster featuring good old-fashioned up-and-down hills, has been one of Cedar Point's most popular coasters since it opened. It was the first hypercoaster, and from its beachside location, Lake Erie seems a long way down. Trains leave the lift and plunge 194 feet to the sand at a 60-degree angle, reaching speeds of more than 72 mph. Outbound, the ride includes a second tall, twisted power dive into a tunnel followed by a low-profile speed bump whose sustained negative-G launch is beyond description. A fast, banked pretzel turnaround sends the train home over a series of rabbit hops, each of which rockets riders off their seats. For many enthusiasts, *Magnum* is their No. 1 steel coaster. One ride and you'll most likely agree.

Mantis (1996)—*steel-track stand-up looper, 145 feet high, 3,900-foot run:* When it was built, *Mantis* was the world's biggest stand-up coaster. This ride is famous for its ultra-strong positive-Gs, due to the exaggerated size of its drops and elements. Inversions include a 119-foot tall vertical loop, a diving loop, an inclined (tilted) loop, and a corkscrew.

Mean Streak (1991)—*wood-track twister, 160 feet high, 5,427-foot run:* A structurally beautiful coaster, *Mean Streak* is similar to the *Texas Giant* at Six Flags Over Texas. *Mean Streak* riders are treated to a 155-foot first drop and numerous fast turns and drops as the track weaves a turbulent path through the structurework.

Raptor (1994)—*steel-track inverted looper, 137 feet high, 3,790-foot run:* This ride's layout is more spread out than most inverteds that came before it. *Raptor*'s green track and supports coil high above Cedar Point's main midway, allowing non-riders to enjoy the train's aerial acrobatics.

Geauga Lake, Aurora (near Cleveland)

Big Dipper (1926)—*wood-track out-and-back, 65 feet high, 2,680-foot run:* This coaster looks so good and rides so well, you won't believe it's been entertaining park patrons for more than 70 years (an extensive rebuild in 1980 helped). If you want a textbook example of a Golden Age classic in terms of looks and ride quality, this is it. John Miller's large hills deliver an exquisite ride that will have you floating over its numerous peaks.

Double Loop (1977)—*steel-track oval looper, 95 feet high, 1,800-foot run:* Geauga's first major steel coaster and the first anywhere in the U.S. to feature two vertical loops.

Raging Wolf Bobs (1988)—*wood-track twister, 80 feet high, 3,426-foot run:* The spirit of Chicago's famed *Bobs* roller coaster lives! Though not intended to be a faithful replica of the Riverview *Bobs,* Geauga's incarnation did draw upon many of the original *Bobs'* characteristics: the water-wings track plan; multi-level trackage in the "neck" of the ride; snappy turnarounds; and trailered trains which deftly slice their way through serpentine trackage. In place of the original's famed, ferocious first-drop "fan" turn is a heavily banked turnaround which jettisons trains toward the first

The coaster centerpiece of Cedar Point is the new *Mean Streak,* whose P.T.C. trains eat up a mile of track before the ride is over, making this coaster the second-longest wood coaster ride in the world—but the longest with only one lift hill. This scene, taken from the ride's mid-course safety blocking brake section, shows the queue line, which is surrounded by the coaster. *Terry Lind*

The *Big Dipper* at Geauga Lake near Cleveland is another John Miller work of art. For the 1980 season, the entire ride had been rebuilt in kind using new lumber and rails, but the park thankfully resisted temptation to do any extensive deviation that would have drastically altered its original track plan. The park's *Double Loop* coaster is at upper left. *Mike Schafer*

A look into the "neck" of the *Raging Wolf Bobs* at Geauga Lake reveals the ride's twisted nature, adopted from its mentor, the Riverview Park *Bobs*. Except for the flat turn off the lift hill (center background) and higher water-wing turns, the *Raging Wolf Bobs* loosely follows the original ride's design. *Mike Schafer*

water-wing turnaround. From there it's back-and-forth, under, around, and through in a blur of passing timbers that leaves riders disoriented—an essential quality of the original *Bobs*.

Serial Thriller (1998)—*steel-track inverted looper:* Like *The Great Nor'easter* on Morey's Pier (Wildwood, New Jersey), riders sit in ski lift-like vehicles (two-abreast) with their feet dangling. This $10 million version is a bit taller and has additional inversions.

Paramount's Kings Island, Cincinnati

Adventure Express—*steel-track scenic railway, 63 feet high, 2,963-foot run:* Many consider this to be the best scenic railway-type coaster in the U.S. Built on a sloping hillside, trains leave the station and plunge headlong into the valley before climbing one of two lifts. The unusually fast ride is packed with tight turns, tunnels, quick and unpredictable direction changes, and other surprises.

Beast (1978)—*wood-track out-and-back/twister, 135 feet high, 7,400-foot run:* As the world's longest wooden roller coaster featuring a number of unusual characteristics, the *Beast* has become a legend in its own time. It consistently ranks among the all-time favorite coasters ever; the *Beast* is remarkable, awesome—and controversial. Purists pooh-pooh its lack of traditional, up-and-down hills

and steep drops. Nonetheless, the first drop is breathtaking because it dives into *The Tunnel That's Too Small for the Coaster Train!* Beyond, the ride becomes an over-testosteroned scenic railway run amok. The track literally winds downhill, tunneling in and out of the hillside, so that the train gains relentless speed. Suddenly, the *Beast* changes personality as the train enters the second lift hill. Purists dismiss this as an unwanted interruption in the ride's otherwise fast pacing, while others claim the *clank, clank, clank* up the lift sets an ominous tone for the impending *Beast*'s "Lair." The 141-foot, 45-degree approach to the lair—in reality a covered helix—allows trains to gather paralyzing speed. The blurring trip through the timberlined tunnel borders on the horrific: decapitation seems imminent, and if it's not *your* head, surely someone else's will end up in your lap.

Beastie (1972)—*wood-track oval/figure-eight, 38 feet high, 1,350-foot run:* Like its big brother (previous entry), this junior woodie features a tunnel at the bottom of the first drop. This is a standardized P.T.C. ride which has kin at other U.S. and Canadian parks.

King Cobra (1984)—*steel-track stand-up looper, 95 feet high, 2,230-foot run:* *King Cobra* was the first stand-up coaster in the U.S. Its first drop leads to a vertical loop—buckling the knees of standing riders—while a follow-up banked helix has you standing sideways.

Kings Island's *Beastie* is a John Allen "junior" coaster that's great for up-and-coming coaster riders, and veterans like it too. Originally named *Scooby Doo*, the ride was rechristened *Beastie* when it acquired the tunnel at the bottom of the first drop—just like its big brother across the park. *Mike Schafer*

Racer (1972)—*wood-track out-and-back racer, 88 feet high, 3,415-foot run, each track:* There is much reverence for the *Racer*, credited for ushering in the coaster boom that continues more than a quarter century later. Situated in Kings Island's Coney Island section (dedicated to the memory of the defunct Cincinnati park of that name), the magnificent *Racer* basks in ongoing popularity—there's always a big crowd of enthusiastic folks of all ages waiting to board. The *Racer* delivers a fast-paced, exhilarating ride, and passengers on the red and blue trains cheer and yell with delight all the way to the finish line.

Top Gun (1993)—*steel-track suspended, 100 feet high, 2,352-foot run:* One of the fastest suspended coasters, *Top Gun* is built above and within one of Kings Island's secluded valleys. The ride is

For more than 20 years, the *Beast* at Cincinnati's Kings Island has been a remarkably popular ride, and for that same period, its record length of 7,400 feet has remained unbroken. Separated by a mid-ride lift hill, there are two "sides" to the *Beast*—and this look from the second lift reveals the "badder" of the two. *Beast* trains gain demonic speed as they shoot along the incline leading to the ride's harrowing helix, the opening to which is only a foot tall—or so it appears. *Mike Schafer*

characterized by quick, swooping turns and directional changes. The swinging trains simulate flight in a jet fighter.

Vortex (1987)—*steel-track looper, 148 feet high, 3,800-foot run:* A pioneer in the field of the mega-steel coaster technology which emerged in the late 1980s, *Vortex* features a track layout that is even more twisted than your telephone cord (if that's possible), full of vertical loops, spirals, barrel-rolls, and a boomerang track section.

Stricker's Grove, Ross (near Cincinnati)

Teddy Bear—*wood-track junior oval:* Park owner Ralph Stricker built this small ride for the younger park patrons.

Tornado (1993)—*wood-track twister, 55 feet high, 2,080-foot run:* Inspired by the defunct *Mighty Lightnin'* at Rocky Glen Park (Moosic, Pennsylvania), Ralph Stricker built his own wooden version. The result is a highly entertaining medium-sized thriller that really packs a punch. Stricker's Grove is a private picnic park, not open to the public.

Wyandot Lake, Powell (near Columbus)

Sea Dragon—*wood-track oval/figure-eight:* This model is another example of a "catalog" P.T.C. junior coaster and is similar to the *Comet* at Waldameer Park (Pennsylvania), the *Beastie* at Kings Island (Ohio), and other parks.

OKLAHOMA
Bell's Amusement Park, Tulsa

Zingo (1968)—*wood-track out-and-back, 72 feet high, 2,560-foot run:* Not many wooden coasters were constructed at the end of the 1960s, but this is one of them, and it's a beautiful ride. Coaster connoisseurs will recognize John Allen hallmarks: a small "swoop turn" off the chain lift leading to the first drop, high hills, and smooth drops. Because it drops below ground level, the third hill on *Zingo* is the longest (as is the case on other John Allen coasters), at 86 feet.

Frontier City, Oklahoma City

Silver Bullet (1979)—*steel-track looper, 83 feet high, 1,942-foot run:* This compact looper operated in Texas and Maryland before settling in at Frontier City in 1986. The *Bullet* is nearly identical to the Viper at AstroWorld in Texas.

Wildcat (1968)—*wood-track out-and-back with steel structurework, 75 feet high, 2,653-foot run:* In 1991, Frontier City rescued the old

Fairyland Park (Kansas City) *Wildcat* from certain doom. The park relocated the ride, had the layout reconfigured, and unleashed a "new" *Wildcat* that is quite different from its original form, with a turbulent new fan turn and odd, high sections of track.

WISCONSIN
Big Chief Kart & Coaster World, Wisconsin Dells

Cyclops (1995)—*wood-track twister, 90 feet high, 1,680-foot run:* Built on a hillside, *Cyclops'* brief but speedy circuit features a curving drop off the chain lift, several quick turns and a surprisingly steep, 75-foot vertical finale drop/turn over a cliff.

Pegasus (1996)—*wood-track junior twister, 56 feet high, 1,278-foot run:* *Pegasus* is an unusual junior twister with gentle hills and turns. This is a perfect starter coaster for the young enthusiasts, or for those not quite ready for the wildness of *Cyclops* or *Zeus*.

Zeus (1997)—*wood-track out-and-back, 90 feet high, 2,500-foot run:* Big Chief's third woodie in as many years, *Zeus* thrills riders with a steep first drop and a series of low-G speed hills and double-dips. A fast, banked turnaround lies in the trees at the far end of the course. As with most coasters, *Zeus* is a mysterious night ride, especially since everything but the lift is hidden, unlighted, within a dense forest.

Kings Island's *King Cobra* created quite a sensation when it opened—as the first stand-up coaster in the U.S. You've never really experienced New Age coastering until you've stood up through a vertical loop, as these 24 bravados are doing on Independence Day, 1990. *David P. Oroszi*

Save for a portable coaster at Wisconsin Dells' Riverview Park, the state was essentially coasterless for all of the 1980s and half of the 1990s. Then along came *Cyclops* and *Zeus* at a new *go-cart* park at the Dells, one of Wisconsin's premier entertainment areas. The two coasters stand side by side. It's no myth: they're both topnotch rides. *Jeffrey Seifert*

5

Roller Coasters
of the
WILD WEST

In this concluding chapter of our coast-to-coast coaster guide, we'll show you "how the West was won" in the great Coaster Renaissance of the 1970s. The nucleus of coaster activity in the American West has long been California, whose coasters—both Golden Age and contemporary—have appeared in several Hollywood flicks. In the 1950s horror classic, *Beast From 20,000 Fathoms*, we catch glimpses of Long Beach's renowned *Cyclone Racer* (1930–1968), while in the 1977 thriller *Rollercoaster*, actor Timothy Bottoms contemplates blowing up Magic Mountain's *Revolution* looping coaster. As in the Southland, the American West lost a great number of Golden Agers during the post-World War II decline years, but fortunately a handful survived (and a significant one was revived) and today they operate side by side with a whole new legion of stars.

If there are a centerpiece park and coaster for the American West, they may well be Denver's Lakeside Park and its first-rate *Cyclone* roller coaster. A wonderland of neon and electric lights and Art Deco buildings, family-owned Lakeside has been entertaining fun-seekers since 1908. The 1940 *Cyclone* is a classic in every respect, starting right at its phenomenal boarding station, shown on a July evening in 1982. *Mike Schafer*

San Diego's *Giant Dipper* is the most stunningly revitalized coaster of the renaissance era—and as a Golden Ager, historically significant as well. This front-seat view from aboard one of the *Dipper*'s rip-roaring trains clearly illustrates Prior & Church hallmarks: a compact layout and nary a level, straight piece of track. The restoration work on this coaster is dazzling. *Terry Lind*

ARIZONA
Castles & Coasters, Phoenix

Desert Storm (1991)—*steel-track looper, 90 feet high, 2,000-foot run:* This compact ride features two vertical loops—each threaded by a section of track—and a collection of quick drops and turns.

Patriot (1991)—*steel-track junior, 35 feet high, 700-foot run:* The *Patriot*'s drops and turns are gentle enough for small children.

CALIFORNIA
Belmont Park, San Diego

Giant Dipper (1925)—*wood-track twister, 70 feet high, 2,600-foot run:* The *Giant Dipper* is one of the few remaining examples of the unparalleled designs of Golden Age master Fred Church. Though by no means large by today's standards, the ride manages to pack in more thrills and excitement than modern coasters twice its size. The *Giant Dipper* is loaded with tight swooping drops, rapid changes of direction, and plenty of subtle, hidden surprises, and its flanged-wheel trains make for a fast, smooth ride. This exquisite coaster, briefly named *Earthquake*, closed along with the park in 1976 and would have faded into oblivion had it not been for the admirable efforts of the Save The Coaster Committee, which was instrumental in having it declared a National Historic Landmark. Luckily, a partnership called the San Diego Coaster Company was formed, and they miraculously returned the *Giant Dipper* to its former glory.

Disneyland, Anaheim (near Los Angeles)

Big Thunder Mountain Railroad (1979)—*steel-track scenic railway:* For a ride description and photo, see the Walt Disney World entry in Chapter 3.

Gadget's Go Coaster (1993)—*steel-track junior 28 feet high, 679-foot run:* *Gadget's* is a heavily-themed steel coaster.

Matterhorn Bobsled (1959)—*steel-track scenic railway, 80 feet high, 2,037 feet and 2,134 feet:* This coaster introduced the tubular steel-track format which today dominates coaster-dom. As the name implies, the *Matterhorn* is themed as a bobsled and is really two separate coasters intertwined within the confines of the scaled-down Matterhorn peak (of Switzerland fame) which looms over the park. Because the single cars duck in and out of the mountainside, riders can never really be sure where they're headed, which makes for an entertaining ride that concludes with a "splash down."

Space Mountain (1977)—*steel-track twister, 3,500-foot run:* This *Space Mountain* is nearly identical to its prototype at Walt Disney World in Florida; see Chapter 3 for a ride description.

Marine World Africa USA, Vallejo

Kong (1995)—*steel-track inverted looper, 104 feet high, 2,171-foot run:* When Premier Parks purchased Marine World and decided to install a selection of thrill rides, this ride was the perfect complement to the *Boomerang* shuttle-loop coaster opening the same year. *Kong* (basically the same ride as *The Great Nor'easter* on Morey's Pier, Wildwood, New Jersey) thrilled riders at Nashville's now-closed Opryland as the *Hangman* for three seasons before migrating west.

Grizzly's rustic appearance contrasts with the high-tech buildings near Paramount's Great America in Santa Clara, California. The *Grizzly* has some P.T.C. traits, such as the "flat" ascents and descents—no surprise, since the *Grizzly* and its three sisters are based on the P.T.C.-designed *Wildcat* that prowled Cincinnati's Coney Island from 1925 to 1970. *Otto P. Dobnick*

Southern California's Santa Susana Mountains form an impressive backdrop for an impressive racing coaster, *Colossus*, whose massive structurework looms over Six Flags Magic Mountain and is a landmark along Interstate 5 between Los Angeles and the San Joaquin Valley. Up to six trains ply its 8,650 feet of track. *Otto P. Dobnick*

Home for Santa Cruz's *Big Dipper* is a classic seaside amusement park, complete with a quintessential California beach. The Pacific Ocean is but steps from the boarding station of this Arthur Looff masterpiece, whose first drop and fan turn (this end of photo) bears an uncanny resemblance to Chicago's erstwhile Riverview *Bobs*. *Otto P. Dobnick*

Paramount's Great America, Santa Clara (Bay Area)

Blue Streak (1984)—*steel-track junior, 36 feet high, 1,300-foot run*: This speedy junior ride originally operated at Houston's AstroWorld before relocating to Great America in 1987.

Demon (1976)—*steel-track looper, 95 feet high, 2,300-foot run*: This coaster's life story and ride description are identical to that of its sister at Six Flags Great America near Chicago. See Chapter 4.

Grizzly (1986)—*wood-track twister, 90 feet high, 3,200-foot run*: This ride is one of four incarnations based on the famous *Wildcat* that thrilled riders from 1926 to 1970 at Cincinnati's Coney Island. Having been tamed and somewhat flattened, the California version is relatively mild when compared to its cousins at Kings Dominion (Virginia), Canada's Wonderland, and Australia's Wonderland.

Top Gun (1993)—*steel-track suspended, 100 feet high, 2,260-foot run*: *Top Gun* is an elongated version of *Batman–The Ride* appearing at Six Flags parks.

Vortex (1991)—*steel-track stand-up looper, 91 feet high, 1,950-foot run*: One of the first generation of ultra-smooth stand-up coasters. Elements include a vertical loop, corkscrew, and spiral.

Knott's Berry Farm, Buena Park (near Los Angeles)

Jaguar (1995)—*steel-track junior twister, 65 feet high, 2,700-foot run*: This Mayan-themed coaster winds above the park with gentle

85

Ninja sprawls all over one of the peaks within Magic Mountain park, and the boarding station (tan-roofed building at bottom of photo) is at the top. The track is enveloped by trees and intertwines with a water ride. *Ninja's* main lift hill comes at the end of the ride, at right in the photo. A portion of the *Psyclone* is visible at upper left. *Terry Lind*

drops and turns, and at one point passes through the loop on *Montezooma's Revenge*, a shuttle-loop coaster cousin.

Windjammer (1997)—*steel-track racing looper, 60 feet high, 1,843 feet each track*: This surf-themed coaster consists of two parallel tracks which follow an undulating course with swoops and tight turns, including a single vertical loop on each side.

Santa Cruz Beach Boardwalk, Santa Cruz

Giant Dipper (1924)—*wood-track twister, 70 feet high, 2,640-foot run*: This brilliant coaster has achieved National Historic Landmark status, and with good reason: the *Giant Dipper* is a pristine example of a surviving Golden Age roller coaster. Also, veterans of the late, lamented *Bobs* (1924–1967) at Chicago's Riverview Park will note some interesting similarities in the *Giant Dipper*, not only its first drop into a potent fan curve, but also the ride's compact, twisted-but-sensuous, multi-layered trackage. The *Giant Dipper* exhibits another *Bobs* trait—fast-pacing flanged-wheeled trains. These similarities are more than coincidence. Designer Arthur Looff used Prior & Church patents on the *Giant Dipper*; Frederick Church designed the Riverview *Bobs*. The *Giant Dipper*

is unquestionably among the best in the West! If you visit California and fail to ride the *Giant Dipper*, we're going to have to ask you for a written excuse from your mother.

Scandia Family Fun Center, Ontario (east of Los Angeles)

Scandia Screamer (1995)—*steel-track twister, 90 feet high, 2,600-foot run*: This multi-layered twister surprises first-time riders with steep drops, tight turns, and some unexpected moments of air time.

Six Flags Magic Mountain, Valencia (northwest of Los Angeles)

Batman–The Ride (1994)—*steel-track inverted looper, 105 feet high, 2,700-foot run*: This ride is basically the same as *Batmans* at other Six Flags parks. See Chapter 2, Great Adventure, New Jersey, for a ride description.

Colossus (1978)—*wood-track oval/twister racer, 115 feet high, 4,325 feet per track*: When this mammoth racer first opened, it had a fierce reputation due to excessive negative G-forces. In 1979, the giant was tamed by lowering some hills and raising others. Although much of *Colossus'* bite has been eliminated, it's still an enjoyable ride and is a structural work of art.

Gold Rusher (1971)—*steel-track scenic railway*, 2,690-*foot run:* Magic Mountain's first coaster. The peppy ride's course closely follows the profile of the hills and ravines and features two lifts, plenty of tight turns, spirals, and surprise dips.

Ninja (1988)—*steel-track suspended twister*, 85 *feet high*, 2,700-*foot run:* This impressive suspended coaster's loading station is perched atop one of the park's tallest peaks. A 60-foot lift takes the train farther up to the first drop, and from there it's a wild ride down the mountain, swooping through the trees, narrowly missing supports, and making a final plunge down to the surface of a lagoon. A long lift returns the train to the station.

Psyclone (1991)—*wood-track twister*, 95 *feet high*, 2,970-*foot run:* Psyclone was the third ride fashioned after the Coney Island *Cyclone*, but with some variations. Except for the initial plunge, the rough-and-tumble *Cyclone*-inspired hills have been somewhat flattened and the banking in the turns increased.

Revolution (1976)—*steel-track twister/looper*, 113 *feet high*, 3,457-*foot run:* The first modern coaster to feature a 360-degree vertical loop, the *Revolution* makes wonderful use of mountainous terrain, with graceful dives over hills and into ravines. The *Revolution* starred in the film *Rollercoaster*.

Viper (1990)—*steel-track looper*, 188 *feet high*, 3,830-*foot run:* This enormous ride includes three vertical loops, a boomerang, and a

Even if the coaster was nameless, there's little doubt that *Psyclone* was inspired by the Coney Island *Cyclone*. Compare this first-seat, first-drop view with that of the original in Chapter 2. Nonetheless, *Psyclone*'s curves are more heavily banked, which reduces lateral forces on riders, so the feel that you're going to be torn sideways out of the train is considerably less than on the Coney original. *Terry Lind*

Wrapped around a forested hill, Magic Mountain's *Revolution* is one of the ultimate terrain coasters and in some ways could be considered a high-speed scenic railway. It has but one inversion—a vertical loop—which is enhanced by a long "speedway" approach that follows a special braking section. *Otto P. Dobnick*

Two of new Elitch Gardens' coasters are visible in this 1996 scene which looks westward toward the Front Range of the Colorado Rockies. Dominating the park is *Twister II*, which bears a family resemblance to the original [*Mister*] *Twister* (Chapter 1), which as this volume went to press was still standing, moribund, at the old Elitch site near Lakeside Park. *Twister II* has some significant differences, yet more than one coaster enthusiast felt that *Twister II* offered an outstanding ride. In the foreground is the *Sidewinder*, a shuttle-loop coaster. *Otto P. Dobnick*

pair of corkscrews. Situated on a hill overlooking the park, its coiling structure appears quite imposing.

Flashback (*1985*)—*steel-track twister, 86 feet high, 1,900-foot run:* This is the only coaster of its type in the U.S., and once you see it in action, you'll know why. Arranged in a giant, stacked "Z" pattern, the track abruptly drop-twists such that the trains "dive bomb" to another level. The track is so convoluted in places that, from a rider's perspective, you won't believe that the train can successfully negotiate it. This ride debuted at Great America (Chicago) as the *Z-Force* and was moved to Six Flags Over Georgia in 1988; Magic Mountain got it in 1992.

COLORADO
Elitch Gardens, Denver

Twister II (*1995*)—*wood-track twister, 100 feet high, 3,400-foot run:* Though *Twister II* shares a similar footprint with the original John Allen-designed masterpiece, [*Mister*] *Twister* at the old Elitch park site, the ride at the new park location is in no way a duplicate. *Twister II* thrills its riders with impressive speed, lateral jolts, and a tunneled swoop turn that'll scare the—uh—daylights out of you. This ride has a "controlled" feel to it, where the original was notorious for its unpredictable, relentless nature and unchecked speeds. Nothing can replace *Twister*, but *Twister II* is an outstanding ride on its own and a worthy successor to one of the best wooden roller coasters ever designed.

Mind Eraser (*1997*)—*steel-track inverted looper, 100 feet high, 2,172-foot run:* See description for the sister *Mind Eraser* at Riverside Park, Massachusetts, Chapter 2.

Lakeside Park, Denver

Cyclone (*1940*)—*wood-track twister/out-and-back, 80 feet high, 2,800-foot run:* The *Cyclone* is one of the all-time great treasures of coasterdom, and it's situated in one of the most beautiful, traditional amusement parks ever. As you approach the *Cyclone's*

Lakeside's *Cyclone* is a combination twister and out-and-back with immaculately maintained, museum-quality rolling stock. These *Cyclone* riders have just experienced the twister segment of the ride and are plunging into the out-and-back section along Lake Rhoda, named for the original park owner's daughter, who now operates Lakeside with loving care. *Mike Schafer*

Art Deco loading station, you'll think you've stepped right back into the 1940s. And when one of the vintage trains rolls in for loading, you'll know you're in for something special. Following a quick trip through the tunnel and the clankety climb up the lift hill, the train makes a dive-bomb curve into the first drop. The track climbs, swoops, and circles repeatedly before its out-and-back dash along Lake Rhoda. Before you know it, you're back home in the *Cyclone's* palace of a boarding station.

Coaster Technology

HOW DO COASTER TRAINS STAY ON THE TRACK?

Many early coaster trains rode the rails much like a regular railway train, on flanged wheels only. The flanges kept the wheels on the rails—as long as hills and curves were gentle. Enter side-friction tracking: coaster cars were equipped with non-flanged running wheels, which rode on iron or steel strap rails bolted to wood, and side-friction wheels which faced outward, riding against side boards which kept the cars on course. This turn-of-the-century technology allowed coaster cars to make fast, sharp turns and virtually eliminated derailments. Side-friction tracking became widely accepted, despite some drawbacks, mainly somewhat wobbly tracking. At least one existing U.S. coaster—*Leap-the-Dips* at Lakemont Park in Altoona, Pennsylvania—employs side-friction track and cars.

With the demand for more-daring coasters on the upswing, coaster builders had to come up with a wheel arrangement that not only enabled cars to track well through convoluted trackage, but also kept them from lifting off the track on hilltops. The answer was to devise a scheme that virtually locked coaster cars to the track. Such designs made their appearance in the nineteenth century, but it wasn't until John Miller patented the "underfriction" wheel in 1912 that the concept caught on in a big way.

This close-up view of a coaster train on *Vortex* at Carowinds park in North Carolina clearly illustrates coaster-wheel technology pioneered by Miller—a technology that applies to both wood- and tubular steel-track coasters. The largest of the visible wheels are the running wheels, which support most of the weight of the coaster train, even when it is upside down (centrifugal forces keep the weight of the train against the running wheels within a loop). Opposite the running wheels, on the underside of the rail, are the underfriction wheels. Not only do they serve as a backup in the event that a train passes through a loop too slowly, keeping it from dropping off the tracks, but they also keep trains from lifting off the tracks where negative G-forces are high, such as the apex of a hill. Perpendicular to the running and underfriction wheels are the side-friction wheels, which stabilize lateral motion.

IDAHO
Silverwood, Athol

Timber Terror (1996)—*wood-track out-and-back, 85 feet high, 2,700-foot run:* Briefly known as the *Grizzly*, the *Timber Terror* is the Northwest's first wooden coaster in more than 35 years. This bear runs its course at breakneck speed, subjecting riders to steep drops, endless doses of floating air time, and a rollicking lateral-G helix finale.

Gravity Defying Corkscrew (1975)—*steel-track corkscrew, 70 feet high, 1,250-foot run:* This is the very first *Corkscrew* prototype, built for Knott's Berry Farm in 1975 and *the* ride which kicked off the era of the modern looping coaster. It was moved to Idaho in 1990.

NEVADA
Buffalo Bill's Hotel & Casino, Primm

Desperado (1994)—*steel-track hypercoaster, 209 feet high, 5,843-foot run:* *Desperado* rules this desert kingdom. The enormous ride's station is *inside* the casino, and the lift exits through a hole in the roof! Trains ascend 209 feet above the desert floor and then power dive 225 feet into an underground tunnel at a 60-degree angle. A wickedly steep climb and turn set the train up for a swooping drop to the ground followed by three elevated camelbacks which provide wonderfully violent, sustained negative Gs. An enclosed upward spiral completes this outrageous coaster. *Desperado* is currently tied with Kennywood's *Steel Phantom* as having the longest drop in North America.

New York New York Hotel & Casino, Las Vegas

Manhattan Express (1997)—*steel-track looper, 203 feet high, 4,777-foot run:* TOGO of Japan had the daunting task of building an enormous roller coaster on the casino roof and around the property's perimeter. The result is a thrilling coaster that struts its stuff high above the excitement of the Las Vegas Strip. The Coney Island-themed ride begins inside a "subway station" in the casino. The yellow trains travel outside, climb a 203-foot-high lift, and suddenly drop 144 feet. A quick ascent is followed by a 144-foot plunge right over the valet entrance. Next, the train leaps onto the casino roof (in full view of Las Vegas crowds) and enters a tight mass of twisted trackage before dropping through a hole in the roof back to the station.

Grand Slam Canyon, Las Vegas

Canyon Blaster (1993)—*steel-track corkscrew/looper, 99 feet high, 2,423-foot run:* This ride is located under a pink glass dome and intertwines with a number of other attractions. For it's finale, the *Blaster* negotiates a wild spiral, tunneling through a man-made stone mountain.

91

Desperado at Buffalo Bill's Hotel & Casino in Primm is a hypercoaster in every sense of the word, and one of several new coasters to swoop in on Nevada—long a coasterless state. *Desperado*'s loading station is inside the casino, but the rest of the coaster flounces all over the place outside the complex. An outrageous ride? You betcha! *Scott Rutherford*

MGM Grand Adventures, Las Vegas

Lightning Bolt (1993)—*steel-track twister, approx. 25 feet high:* When originally opened, this ride was enclosed in a building and had an outer space theme. For the 1998 season, it was moved outdoors and enlarged with a second lift and additional track.

Stratosphere Hotel & Casino, Las Vegas

High Roller (1996)—*steel-track oval:* Perched atop the amazing Stratosphere Tower (the tallest building west of the Mississippi), the *High Roller* is a small non-looping steel coaster that wraps around the outside of the structure 909 feet above the Strip. Though not a huge ride, the fact that you're in a moving train 90 stories in the air more than compensates. Not for the faint-hearted.

OREGON
Enchanted Forest, Turner

Ice Mountain Bobsled (1982)—*steel-track twister, 2,000-foot run:* This unusual ride began as an Alpine Slide but morphed into a steel terrain coaster. The *Bobsled* features two lifts which take the trains up a mountainside and release them into a wild mixture of banked turns and hills.

UTAH
Lagoon Park and Pioneer Village, Farmington
(between Salt Lake City and Ogden)

Colossal Fire Dragon (1982)—*steel-track looper, 85 feet high, 2,800-foot run:* This ride made its debut during Germany's 1982 Oktoberfest, was purchased by Lagoon, and opened in Utah in 1983. Highlights include two vertical loops and multiple positive-G spirals.

Roller Coaster (1921)—*wood-track twister, 60 feet high, 2,598-foot run:* An entertaining John Miller Golden Ager with camelback hills, rapid flat turns, and lively air time. *Roller Coaster* has gone through a number of rebuilds during its long life, the most recent occurring in 1996.

WASHINGTON
Enchanted Village, Federal Way

Wild Thing (1984)—*steel-track looper, 80 feet high, 1,565-foot run: Wild Thing* is a quick ride featuring one vertical loop and a pair of corkscrews. It was originally built for Rhode Island's Rocky Point Park but moved to Washington in 1997.

Western Washington Fair, Puyallup

Roller Coaster (1935)—*wood-track twister, 52 feet high, 2,650-foot run:* This intriguing woodie began life as a side-friction coaster. After a 1949 fire, it was converted to a flanged-wheel/underfriction operation. It is the only roller coaster in the world still using Prior & Church rolling stock (acquired from the defunct Happyland *Giant Dipper* in Vancouver, Washington). These splendid single-seat articulated trains traverse the tight turns and multi-leveled course with the grace of gazelles. *Roller Coaster* only operates two weeks out of each year, during the fair. A ride aboard this vintage classic is well worth the precise planning required to ride it.

Members of the American Coaster Enthusiasts ham it up as the vintage P.&C. train of Western Washington Fair's *Roller Coaster* inches its way up the chain lift. Clearly visible are the train's flanged wheels, which obviate the need for side-friction wheels (though not underfriction wheels) while providing exceptional tracking quality. *Terry Lind*

6

Thrill Guide
to America's Best ROLLER COASTERS

THE NON-OFFICIAL TOP 20 COASTERS YOU REALLY OUGHTA CHECK OUT

It's the question most often asked of coaster fans: Which roller coaster is the best? Sorry folks, but there really isn't one "correct" answer. Like a lot of things people have a passion for—food, movies, and spouses, among many others—it's a matter of personal taste. Ask 100 ardent coaster fans to name their 10 favorites, and you'll likely get 100 different lists!

Nonetheless, here is a list of not only the most-revered and favored coasters that were operating as this book went to press, but also some you'll want to sample for their historical significance or design quirks. The list provides a cross section of coaster types, from scenic railways to wild and woolly megacoasters, wood and steel. Some caveats, though. . .

First and foremost (and you've probably all heard this in regard to other aspects of pleasure), biggest is definitely not always bestest. Although the list does include some record-breakers as to both height and track length, those two items alone do not necessarily a great coaster make. Unfortunately, some new megacoasters have become little more than endurance tests. Often, we've seen coaster fans line up to ride a new megacoaster, get their ride, and then spend the rest of the day repeat-riding the park's other, smaller, more rideable coasters.

So what is the key to success? A coaster that offers a nifty combination of ride elements (e.g., air time, tight turns, great dips) and rideability—in other words, a coaster you could enjoy repeatedly without stressing out. These considerations knock out a number of new record-breakers, although certainly there are coaster fans who *do* indeed like masochistic extremes. We suspect, though, that the bulk of those reading this book do not fall into that category, and our list takes that into consideration.

Also keep in mind that several new coasters had just opened or were about to open as this book was being prepared and were too new to fully compile enough rider experiences for a popularity report. Such was the case for such rides as the new-but-very-promising *Wildcat* at Hersheypark and the *Steel Force* at Dorney Park, both in Pennsylvania (possibly *the* best state for coastering, by the way).

And finally, we think that *all* coasters are fun, whether or not they're on this list. So, hunt 'em all and ride 'em all, whether they're featured in this book (and list) or not!

1. *Beast*, **PARAMOUNT'S KINGS ISLAND, CINCINNATI, OHIO**

Since its opening in 1978, the *Beast*—with its 7,400 feet of track—has been the longest operating wooden roller coaster in the world and in various surveys has consistently ranked as the first-choice woodie among coaster fans.

2. *Cyclone*, **ASTROLAND AT CONEY ISLAND, BROOKLYN, NEW YORK**

One of the most longtime famous roller coasters in one of the most famous amusement areas in the world. The *Cyclone's* hefty trains—which have carried Charles Lindbergh, the cast of the TV sitcom *Taxi*, and other notables—ride out grinding turns and nonstop action. The favorite of this book's co-author, Scott Rutherford.

3. *Thunderbolt*, **KENNYWOOD PARK, WEST MIFFLIN (PITTSBURGH), PENNSYLVANIA**

Author Schafer's favorite currently operating coaster, the dual-personality *Thunderbolt* (with half built in 1924 and half in 1968) is yet another ride that consistently rates very high among veteran coaster fans, and it's in one of America's two best traditional amusement parks.

4. *Magnum XL-200*, **CEDAR POINT, SANDUSKY, OHIO**

Another "top of the list" favorite by veteran coaster fans, you'll feel like you're on top of the world on *Magnum*, the world's first steel "hypercoaster."

5. *Texas Giant*, **SIX FLAGS OVER TEXAS, ARLINGTON (DALLAS/FORT WORTH)**

Huge, Texas-size woodie. A wild and wicked twister loaded with good drops, endless turns, and killer speed. Frantic finale leaves you shaking and yet wanting more.

6. *Racer*, **PARAMOUNT'S KINGS ISLAND, CINCINNATI, OHIO**

The genesis ride of the roller coaster renaissance that began in 1972. For just plain, all-American whoop 'n' holler fun, ride and savor this beauty.

7. *Phoenix*, **KNOEBEL'S GROVE, ELYSBURG, PENNSYLVANIA**

For a textbook example of incredible air time and rip-em-from-the-tracks turns, visit this resurrected classic.

8. *Alpengeist*, **BUSCH GARDENS WILLIAMSBURG, WILLIAMSBURG, VIRGINIA**

One of the best new inverted coaster experiences to come along! *Alpengeist* yanks you from the sky into deep valleys. This steelie gets the vote for most powerful.

9. *Georgia Cyclone*, **SIX FLAGS OVER GEORGIA, ATLANTA**

The best of the *Cyclone* clones, the Georgia version features yank-you-out-of-your-seat drops and fast turns. If you've ridden the Coney original, a ride on the *Georgia Cyclone* will graphically illustrate New Age adaptation of a time-proven design.

10. *Timber Wolf*, **WORLDS OF FUN, KANSAS CITY, MISSOURI**

A New Age woodie often highly rated by coaster fans. Ride this to see why size isn't everything.

11. *Mind Bender*, **SIX FLAGS OVER GEORGIA, ATLANTA**

Let this steelie's smooth, swooping, sensuous track layout exhilarate you. The vertical loops are ecstasy, not brutality.

12. *Racer*, **KENNYWOOD PARK, WEST MIFFLIN (PITTSBURGH), PENNSYLVANIA**

Quite possibly one of the most fun-filled, vintage coasters operating. Kennywood's *Racer* easily offers the most-effective racing experience, with paralleling trains so close you can "high five" your opponent train's passengers.

13. *Big Bad Wolf*, **BUSCH GARDENS WILLIAMSBURG, WILLIAMSBURG, VIRGINIA**

For an unforgettable ride on one of the few suspended coasters in America, let the *Big Bad Wolf* give you a chase. The final drop down to the river's surface is one of the scariest moments on any operating coaster.

14. *Giant Dipper*, **SANTA CRUZ BEACH BOARDWALK, SANTA CRUZ, CALIFORNIA**

Ride the *Giant Dipper* to see what a classic Golden Age beachside twister is all about, and at the same time learn about fan turns, flanged-wheel trains, and infinite rideability.

15. *Giant Dipper*, **BELMONT PARK, SAN DIEGO, CALIFORNIA**

Preservation is the key here. Belmont's *Giant Dipper* illustrates that coasters have historical and architectural significance; one of the few remaining Fred Church classics.

16. *Comet*, **THE GREAT ESCAPE, LAKE GEORGE, NEW YORK**

The best operating oval/out-and-back. Unmitigated speed and lots of air time. Pure fun.

17. *Dragon Coaster*, **PLAYLAND PARK, RYE, NEW YORK**

An architectural masterpiece from the ticket booth on up. This Fred Church work of art features a complex, multi-level track layout that—with *Dragon's* flanged-wheel trains—provides momentum all the way to the brake run.

18. *Adventure Express*, PARAMOUNT'S KINGS ISLAND, CINCINNATI, OHIO

If you're going to experience a mine train coaster, this is perhaps the best one ever devised.

19. *Big Dipper*, GEAUGA LAKE, AURORA (CLEVELAND), OHIO

No coaster list of this nature would be complete without a John Miller-designed classic of the Golden Age. With its numerous parabolic hills, the *Big Dipper* screams "John Miller-r-r-r!" with every down-to-the-ground dip.

20. *Steel Phantom*, KENNYWOOD PARK, WEST MIFFLIN (PITTSBURGH), PENNSYLVANIA

You want record-breakers? As this book goes to press, the *Steel Phantom* is America's fastest coaster (87 mph), and is tied with the *Desperado* (Nevada) as having the longest drop, 225 feet.

APPENDIX: COASTER GLOSSARY

AIR TIME: A highly favored result of a negative G-force, usually occurring at hill tops, that lifts riders from their seats.

BANKED TURN: A curve in which the track is significantly banked to reduce stress on riders and on the track itself.

BOBSLED COASTER: A coaster that features semi-circular trough-like track without rails. The coaster cars or trains have special, angled, rotating wheel sets which allow the cars or trains to flow through a winding track course like a bobsled.

BOOMERANG: A looping track element in which a coaster train exits a double loop section in the opposite direction it entered, coming back on itself.

BRAKE RUN: A section of track equipped with brakes for slowing and stopping trains.

CORKSCREW: A popular element found in several tubular steel-track coasters in which the track "barrel rolls," turning riders upside down twice.

FAN TURN: A wide turnaround—usually 180 degrees or so—in which the whole turn-around (verus just the track) is banked. Lateral forces on fan curves tend to thrust riders to one side and make it feel as though the train may rip from the tracks.

FIGURE-EIGHT: A coaster with a track plan resembling—if you were to view it from straight overhead—a figure eight.

G-FORCE: Gravitational force, either negative or positive, exerted on coaster riders.

HELIX: A section of track that circles upon itself at least once, either ascending or descending in the process.

HYPERCOASTER: A non-inversion coaster of extreme size. To make "hypercoaster"class, the lift hill must be more than 200 feet high and/or one of its drops must exceed 200 feet.

INVERSION: A ride element that turns riders upside down in one manner or another with vertical loops, corkscrews, boomerangs, etc.

INVERTED COASTER: A close cousin to the suspended coaster, an inverted coaster's track is—like the suspended coaster—above the train, but the train's cars are rigidly attached to the bogies (wheel sets) and do not swing.

LAP BAR: The bar that is lowered and locked over the laps of seated riders to keep them in the coaster cars.

LIFT HILL (ALSO "CHAIN LIFT"): A hill up which coaster cars or trains are hauled, usually via a motorized chain. It is usually, but not always, the first hill on a coaster, and a coaster may have more than one lift hill.

N.A.D.: National Amusement Devices, a longtime manufacturer of park rides, best known for its rolling stock—the "Cadillac" of coaster trains.

NEGATIVE Gs: A gravitational force which lifts or even thrusts coaster riders out of their seats ("air time").

OUT-AND-BACK: A coaster with a simple layout in which the track heads more or less straight to its outer end, turns, and heads back to the station.

OVAL COASTER: A coaster with a track plan that is circular or oval in nature.

PARABOLIC HILL: A hill in which the track profile (as viewed from the side) maintains a curve on its way down rather than a straight incline.

POSITIVE Gs: A gravitational force occurring at the bottom of a hill, within a heavily banked turn, or inside a loop that increases the "weight" of a coaster rider.

P.T.C.: Philadelphia Toboggan Company (now Philadelphia Toboggan Coasters). One of the most famous and long-lived builders of roller coasters and coaster trains.

SCENIC RAILWAY: A mild-mannered roller coaster featuring a heavily themed environment.

SIDE-FRICTION COASTER: Wood coasters that utilize a trough-like track in which side running boards are used to keep the car—equipped with side-friction wheels—on course.

SHUTTLE LOOP: A point-to-point coaster in which the train is catapulted through a loop element(s).

SPEED BUMP: A low hill following a large drop (to take advantage of train speed) that causes riders to float out of their seats.

STAND-UP COASTER: A coaster which has trains without seats or sides. Rather, riders stand within special safety harnesses mounted on the train-car platforms.

(TUBULAR) STEEL-TRACK COASTER: A new track-fabrication format developed in the late 1950s in which the rails consist entirely of steel tubing, with welded-steel rail supports.

SUSPENDED COASTER: A coaster featuring trains that are *suspended* from wheel assemblies (bogies) via a hinged arrangement, thereby allowing the cars to swing out on curves; track support is overhead. Since the track is not readily visible to riders, suspended coasters create the sensation of acrobatic flying.

TERRAIN (OR "GULLY") COASTER: A coaster that uses undulating or very irregular terrain to its advantage, with drops fitted into ravines, etc.

TRAILERED (COASTER) TRAIN: A train in which the front portion of each car, except the first car, is supported by the rear wheel assembly of the preceding car. Trailered trains tend to flow better over convoluted track.

TWISTER: A coaster with a convoluted track configuration in which the track twists back and forth, around, over, and/or under itself.

WOOD-TRACK COASTER: Traditional coaster-track construction featuring track comprised of laminated wood on which steel strap rails are bolted on the top (running rails), sides (sidefriction rails), and underneath (underfriction rails). Gauge (distance between rails) is maintained by wood cross-members. Wood-track coasters usually also have wood-supporting structure.

INDEX